A TRAVELER'S GUIDE TO

100

EASTERN GREAT LAKES

Lighthouses

Text: Laurie Penrose
Maps: Bill T. Penrose
Photos: Ruth and Bill J. Penrose

Friede Publications

A Traveler's Guide to 100 Eastern Great Lakes Lighthouses
Copyright, 1994, by Laurie Penrose and Bill Penrose

COVER DESIGN: Boyer Pennington Studios, Ltd.

Friede Publications
2339 Venezia Drive
Davison, Michigan 48423

Printed in the United States of America

First Printing, May 1994

ISBN 0-923 756-09-4

OTHER GUIDEBOOKS BY FRIEDE PUBLICATIONS

———————

A Traveler's Guide to 116 Michigan Lighthouses

A Guide to 199 Michigan Waterfalls

Natural Michigan

More Natural Michigan

Michigan State and National Parks: A Complete Guide

Ultimate Michigan Adventures

Canoeing Michigan Rivers

Fish Michigan — 100 Southern Michigan Lakes

Fish Michigan — 100 Northern Lower Michigan Lakes

Fish Michigan — 100 Upper Peninsula Lakes

CONTENTS

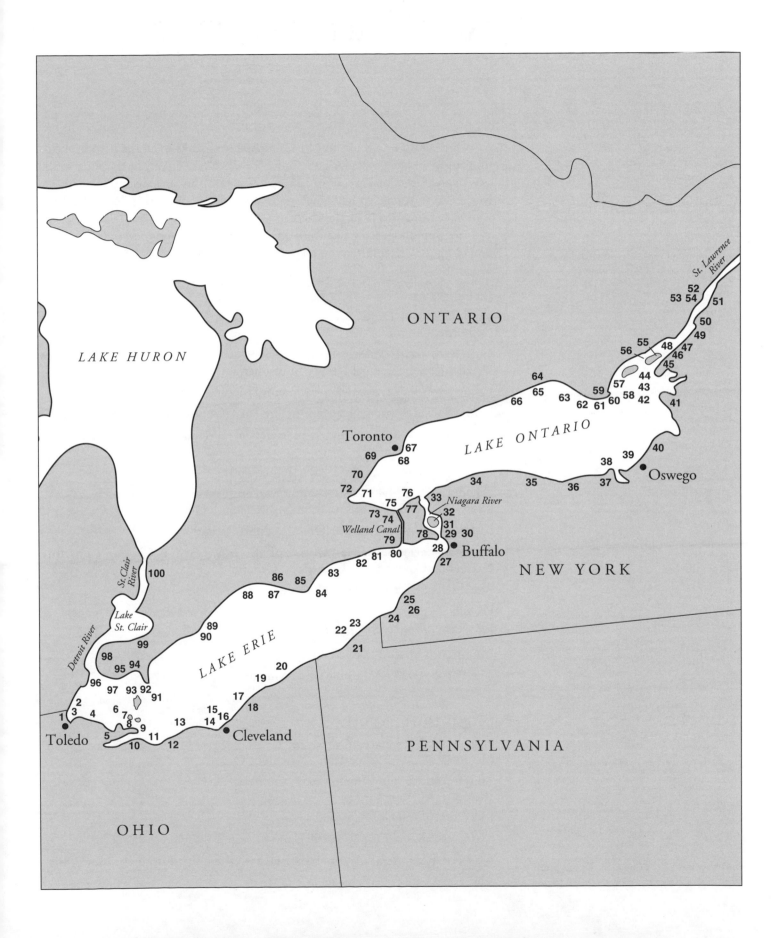

ACKNOWLEDGMENTS

Our family would like to extend our sincere thanks to all the friendly, helpful people we have met along the shores of our Great Lakes. In traveling to the sweetwater lights of Lake Erie, Lake Ontario and the St. Lawrence Seaway, we have been fortunate to have met many new friends on both sides of the lakes who have made this book possible.

We would especially like to thank the following groups and individuals for providing us with information about their local areas.

IN CANADA:

Virginia Anger, *Director and Curator*, Historical and Marine Museum, Port Colborne, Ontario

Gail Benjafield, Valerie Frost and Irmgard Penner, Special Collections Department, Centennial Library, St. Catherines, Ontario

Laurie Fournie, *Curator*, Moore Museum, Mooretown, Ontario

Linda Gula, *Librarian*, Niagara-On-The-Lake (Ontario) Public Library

Don Hanes, Windsor, Ontario, a leader in the club to save the Pelee Island Light

Richard Holl, owner, Pelee Island Trading Post

David Kotin, *History Department Head*, and librarians Gwen Ing and Vicky Casey, Metropolitan Toronto (Ontario) Reference Library

Barbara McAlpine, Oakville (Ontario) Public Library

Captain Larry Schmidt, *Master* of the MV Garden City and Fortune Navigation Company, St. Catherines, Ontario

Ronald Tiessen, Pelee Island Heritage Center

Priscilla Wagner, *Librarian*, Belleville (Ontario) Public Library, main branch

Burlington (Ontario) Public Library

Hamilton (Ontario) Public Library

The Port Burwell (Ontario) Marine Museum

IN THE UNITED STATES:

Gordon D. Amsbary, *Chairman*, Great Lakes Marine and Coast Guard Memorial Museum Association, Ashtabula, Ohio

Annita Andrick and Pamela Green, *Curatorial Assistant*, Erie County Historical Society, Erie, Pennsylvania

Jack Ehmke, Angola, New York

Margaret Falise, *H. Lee White* Marine Museum, Oswego, New York

John Fedak, *Trustee*, Fairport Harbor Historical Society, Fairport Harbor, Ohio

Stan Hale, Lansing, Michigan

FRONT COVER PHOTO: Toledo Harbor Lighthouse, page 3.

Edwin R. Isaly, *Curator*, Lake Erie Islands Historical Society, Put-In-Bay, Ohio

Clyde Koski, Ashtabula, Ohio

Dick Lawson, Dunkirk Lighthouse Museum *Curator*, and Barbara Lawson, *Secretary* of the Dunkirk Historical Lighthouse and Veterans Park Museum, Dunkirk, New York

Martha Long, *Business Director*, and Noelle McFarland, Inland Seas Maritime Museum, for their assistance at the reference library of the Great Lakes Historical Society, Vermilion, Ohio

Jim Marshall, *Local History Department Head*, Toledo-Lucas County Public Library, Toledo, Ohio

Alan Mueller, *Curator*, Charlotte-Genesee Lighthouse Historical Society, Rochester, New York

Rick Novak, *Executive Director*; Linda Marshall, *Executive Secretary*; and Dave Kramer, *Lighthouse Historian*, Lorain Port Authority, Lorain, Ohio

Catherine Olczak, Holt, Michigan

Richard V. Palmer, *Director*, Sodus Bay (New York) Historical Society

Richard A. Rieger, Marblehead, Ohio

Ray and Carol Sotkiewicz, Toledo, Ohio

Mike Vogel and the Buffalo Evening News, Buffalo, New York

Milwaukee (Wisconsin) Public Library Research Services

Old Fort Niagara Association, Youngstown, New York

We would also like to express our sincere gratitude to the men and women of the Canadian Coast Guard and the United States Coast Guard, who were always willing to help, with a special thank you to Mr. E. J. Lea, District Manager; Mr. R. E. Childerhose and Mr. R. Walker of the Canadian Coast Guard Station at Parry Sound, Ontario; Mr. Hugh Jones of the Canadian Coast Guard Station at Prescott, Ontario; PO Martin Fulton of the U.S. Coast Guard Station at Marblehead, Ohio; and BM2 John Freidhoff and BM2 Jeff Long (Ret.) of the U.S. Coast Guard Station at Buffalo, New York.

GREAT LAKES LIGHTHOUSE KEEPERS ASSOCIATION

The Great Lakes Lighthouse Keepers Association is a nonprofit organization "dedicated to the preservation of the lighthouses and the history of the people who kept them."

They offer valuable assistance to local groups trying to save lighthouses, and their own preservation work on the St. Helena Island Lighthouse, near the Straits of Mackinac, has earned the organization national recognition.

By including youth groups in their work, the association is also accomplishing their goal of "developing a new generation of preservationists" who will be ready to take on their own projects.

You can contact the Great Lakes Lighthouse Keepers Association at P.O. Box 580, Allen Park, MI 48101.

Members receive The Beacon, *a quarterly newsletter that includes information about ongoing projects around the lakes, plus firsthand historical accounts of what life was like at the lakes' lighthouses.*

INTRODUCTION

Point Abino Lighthouse

CAUTION

Walking to a lighthouse at the end of a pier or a breakwall can be very pleasant and relaxing during good weather. But when waves wash over these structures, especially during high winds and storms, they become extremely dangerous. Footing is precarious, especially for children. So please use good judgment and caution when visiting those lights. During threatening weather, stay off breakwalls.

The Great Lakes captivate all who travel their shores. For our family, fascination with North America's "inland seas" — and especially their lighthouses — has grown to passion. During the late 1980s and early 1990s we dedicated every available moment to circling Michigan's Great Lakes coastline while researching *A Traveler's Guide to 116 Michigan Lighthouses.*

After the 1992 publication of that book, we stretched beyond the shores of our native state and discovered that lakes Ontario and Erie and their lights have a beauty all their own. From historic Windmill Point Lighthouse, on the banks of the St. Lawrence River, to the light that guards the Lake Erie harbor of Toledo, we have been treated to views of all 100 lighthouses spaced along the Canadian and American shores of those eastern Great Lakes.

After two years and 15,000 miles, we are ready and pleased to share our observations with you. Our primary reason for writing this volume is to make it easier for you and your family to travel to these unique destinations. To enjoy the complete, often-spectacular beauty of these structures, you must visit them.

Most are relatively easy to get to. Some, in fact, are so close to major metropolitan areas such as Toronto, Buffalo, St. Catherines and Cleveland that they are within easy reach of millions of people. Others stand watch on isolated islands far out into the lake. All offer rare glimpses into an important and romantic era on the lakes.

The early 1800s was a time of great expansion along the Great Lakes. After the construction of a series of major canals, thousands of people boarded ships, which carried them over the lakes to new settlements. The Erie Canal, which opened in 1825, connected the Hudson River to Lake Erie. Four years later the Welland Canal opened, and ships had a navigable route between Lake Ontario and Lake Erie. The Rideau Canal, which stretched from the Ottawa River to Lake Ontario, connected the more prosperous and populated areas of inland Canada with the sparsely settled Great Lakes coastline.

As the ship traffic increased, lighthouses were built to facilitate speed and help ensure the safety of passengers. Though the lakes did claim many victims, an incalculable number of accidents and tragedies were averted because dedicated lighthouse keepers hastened to light lamps as twilight approached. As we explored this region, we wondered how many of the beacons had guided and protected our own ancestors 100 years before during their long journey from Cornwall, England, to the iron mines of Negaunee, Michigan.

In the time since, technology has reversed the situation. Now it is the lights that need our protection. Automation — including advanced navigational aids aboard ships — has not only ended the days of lightkeepers, but also some of the lighthouses themselves. Already, some lighthouses that had been cared for and protected for generations have been torn down before they could be saved.

Others, however, have been rescued from such rapid destruction or a slow death at the hands of vandals or through neglect. A few have become part of state, county or provincial parks. Individuals and groups around the lakes have taken on the responsiblity of not only saving others, but also restoring, rebuilding and maintaining the historical treasures. In our lighthouse descriptions, we have included the names of those organizations, when known.

Many lights, however, have no one overseeing their preservation. Their fate lies with all of us.

The Penrose Family
WEST BRANCH, MICHIGAN

COURTESY

Some lighthouses are on private property and are even used as private residences. We urge you to be considerate and respect the rights of their owners. View them from a distance on public land or from the water, and when that is not possible, simply do not attempt to visit at all.

Fresnel lens on display at the Put-In-Bay Historical Society Museum

Manhattan Range Lights

The Manhattan Rear Range Light is a small, square metal room perched atop a 20-foot-high steel skeleton. It has been moved from its original location near the mouth of the Maumee River and re-erected on private property, though not to its original 80-foot height. A metal ladder leads up through the floor of the building, which is surrounded by a railed walkway. The entire structure is pale yellow, with contrasting blue trim around the edge of the walkway. A matching blue roof and ventilator ball top the light.

The Front Range Light, near the shore, is now in two sections. The skeletal base is in pieces, stacked next to the still-intact lantern room and walkway. The square lantern room is painted white, and is covered by a plain metal roof and ventilator.

Both range lights are on private property, but you can view the Rear Range Light from the street.

" The Rear Range has been moved from its original location near the mouth of the Maumee River."

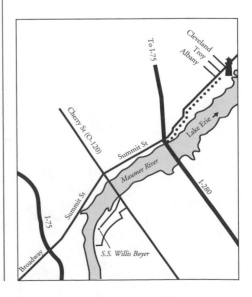

DIRECTIONS: From I-280 in downtown Toledo about 1.5 miles south of I-75, exit onto Summit St. Go northeast on Summit approximately 1.1 miles. As you pass Troy St., on the left, look for the Rear Range Light, behind a cyclone fence on the right.

Also in the downtown area is the retired bulk carrier *S.S. Willis B. Boyer.* Tours are conducted Wednesday through Sunday, April through September. To get to the ship from the Manhattan Range Lights, go southwest on Summit about two miles to Cherry St. Turn left (south) onto Cherry and cross the bridge over the Maumee River. Turn right (west) onto the first road after the bridge and follow it into International Park. For further information call (419) 698-8252.

Turtle Island Lighthouse Ruins

"Turtle Island is no stranger to storms blown up from Lake Erie."

Turtle Island has been important not only to navigators, but also Native Americans and military men. Miami Indians harvested thousands of gull eggs on the island during stopovers on their annual hunting trips to the Maumee area. The island, in fact, takes its name from Miami Chief Little Turtle, whose keen military mind and kindness earned the respect of his American allies in the War of 1812.

Nearly 20 years before, in 1794, the British built a fort on the island in response to an American victory at the Battle of Fallen Timbers on the Maumee River in the Ohio Territory. To shore up their defenses against the American forces to the south, British gunboats regularly patrolled the Detroit River and between Fort Miami (present-day Toledo) and the new fort on Turtle Island. The island fort was abandoned during the War of 1812, and no trace of it remains today.

Turtle Island, which is bisected by the Ohio/Michigan state line, is no stranger to storms blown up from Lake Erie. Once measured at over 6 acres, the island has been reduced to 2 acres by the determined wave action brushing across its beaches. That deterioration also threatened the light after it was first lit in 1831, and so a strong protective breakwall was constructed around the tower. When the Toledo Harbor Light opened in 1904, the Turtle Island Light was abandoned and later sold to a private interest.

Today, it is just an empty shell. The lantern room has vanished, leaving a series of awkward metal poles atop the dark stone tower. A grove of trees has stretched upward to frame the structure in emerald green, and the turquoise waters lap gently at the strip of sand below.

Toledo Harbor Lighthouse

In 1904 a harbor light was put into service that made the lighthouse at Turtle Island obsolete. Jutting out of the water eight miles from the shores of Toledo, the new light was visible up to 16 miles away, had its own fog signal, and was considered the most modern of any structure in the area. Its first keeper, Dell Hayden, arrived from West Sister Island eager to start his position in the state-of-the-art facility.

The light rests on a crib structure nearly 20 feet below the water. Piles of rock that partially surround the light rise almost 10 feet above the water line. A small single-story structure is attached to the much larger, square three-story lighthouse. The house's chocolate-colored brick walls are raised in areas to create slender strips that arch over the third-story windows.

This light's most striking feature is its roof, which instead of traditional flat, straight eaves has a beautiful full-rounded edge. The light tower rises from the center of the dark roof, and its round parapet is enclosed by a steel railing with curved spokes. The lantern room is glazed in dozens of diamond-shaped panes that are also curved, adding to the softness that characterizes this structure.

When the light was automated in 1966, Coast Guard personnel were worried about possible vandalism, so they posted a guard. They dressed a mannequin in a Coast Guardsman's uniform and placed it in the window. The unusual sentry not only successfully discouraged unwanted visitors, but also gave rise to a "Phantom of the Light" legend.

This beautiful light still guides ships into the waters of Toledo Harbor, a duty it has faithfully performed for 90 years.

"The unusual sentry not only discouraged unwanted visitors, but also gave rise to a 'Phantom of the Light' legend."

West Sister Island Lighthouse

"Beautiful West Sister Island is lined with thin sheets of rock stretching slowly out to submerge themselves beneath the turquoise waters of Lake Erie."

Beautiful West Sister Island is eight miles from the Ohio mainland. Its shore is lined with thin sheets of rock stretching slowly out to submerge themselves beneath the turquoise waters of Lake Erie. A sprinkling of gravel beaches also spill out into the water, and behind them the interior of the island is a thick mass of lush greenery, with the pale skeleton of a tree here and there reaching out over the tops of the bushes near the shore.

The first West Sister Island Light was built in 1847, and its thick, 40-foot-tall concrete tower still stands, its pristine whiteness reflected in the blue water below. A small, square window halfway up exposes the emptiness of its dark interior. The parapet and walkway still surround the summit, but the lantern room has been removed.

Old Port Clinton Lighthouse

The Port Clinton Light, originally located on the east bank of the Portage River, has been moved across the river and upstream to a private marina, but you can view it from a nearby drawbridge. Only the upper half of the tower was saved, but it's enough to see the similarity to most range lights on the Canadian side of the lakes — square, with angled sides that rise quickly to meet the parapet. The remains of this tower angle up about 15 feet to where a square, black railing surrounds the octagonal lantern room. The empty lantern room is capped by a metal roof and ventilator ball.

"Only the upper half of the tower was saved."

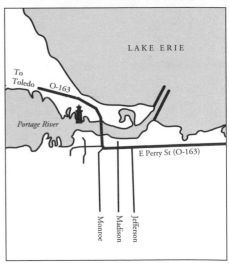

DIRECTIONS: You can get views of this light from the O-163 drawbridge across the Portage River near downtown Port Clinton. It's best to park in the downtown area and walk to the bridge. Follow the sidewalk along the west side of the bridge and look for the light about one block upstream, on the right (north) riverbank.

Green Island Lighthouse

Green Island, about four miles northwest of the tip of Catawba Island, is an imposing mix of high bluffs lining its shore and thick impenetrable forests spreading throughout the interior. In 1854 the first lighthouse to guard these waters was built, with room enough for the keeper and his family, who soon made the island home. Less than 10 years later they were forced to leave under harrowing circumstances.

December 31, 1863, dawned mild and clear, and temperatures hovered unseasonably in the 60s as the keeper Colonel Drake, his wife, and five of their six children readied for a New Year's Eve celebration on the island. One son had decided to attend a party nearby on the main island of South Bass, in Put-In-Bay.

Nature, however, became an unwelcome guest at both parties. By evening a storm had slammed into the area, a storm so intense that the temperature plummeted to 25 degrees below zero in only hours.

Also, for unknown reasons the lighthouse caught fire. The Drake family valiantly fought the flames with buckets of water, but their efforts were futile. As the wood lighthouse burned to the ground, the family huddled outside under a feather mattress, their only remaining shelter.

The Drake son who had gone to South Bass Island stood helplessly as he watched the distant flames dance into the night sky. He desperately hoped his family was alive but could not find out until morning. At sunrise of the first day of the new year, he organized a rescue party and set out to make the treacherous three-mile crossing over thin ice. Yard by yard the men laid planks down, walked to their end, picked them up, and laid them down again, repeating the tortuous process until they finally reached Green Island. There they found that all seven members of the Drake family had survived their night in the sub-zero temperatures.

Today a skeleton tower supports a new, automated light.

South Bass Island Lighthouse

The beautiful South Bass Island Lighthouse was built in 1897 on a rugged piece of shoreline that forms the southwestern tip of the island. The two-story house is expansive, and the keeper and his family must have had a near-fulltime job keeping it ready for surprise visits from lighthouse service inspectors. The brick exterior is interrupted by many windows, including delicately arched attic windows plus a bank of basement windows. A small porch steps down from the back of the structure, and a larger enclosed front porch, supported by brick pillasters, faces the blue expanse of Lake Erie.

The grounds are a mixture of lush green lawns and bands of trees running along the shoreline. Several maples and oaks spread their branches to shade the south wall of the house, and their bright greens contrast nicely with the light-red brick of the nearly 100-year-old structure.

In 1962 the Coast Guard erected a new, white skeleton light, and the old lighthouse was then purchased by Ohio State University. It is currently used as a private residence by researchers, and visitors are not allowed on the property.

The only way to view the light is from the water, and we recommend taking the Miller Boat Line ferry from Catawba Island to Lime Kiln Dock (see map, p. 8). As you approach the island, you can view and photograph the lighthouse, on the left, but by the time the boat docks, the lighthouse is completely hidden by trees.

> " *The keeper and his family must have had a near-fulltime job keeping it ready for surprise visits from lighthouse service inspectors.* "

Perry's Victory and International Peace Memorial

"From an observation deck you can see 60 miles or more on a clear day."

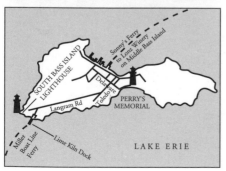

Although not officially a lighthouse, the Perry Victory and International Peace Memorial, at Put-In-Bay on South Bass Island, is recognized by more Lake Erie skippers and visitors than perhaps any other structure on the lake. It can be seen up to 40 miles away and has guided many boaters into the waters near picturesque Put-In-Bay. The 352-foot-tall doric column is topped by a huge bronze urn, and from an observation deck beneath it, you can see 60 miles or more on a clear day. Only yards from the monument's base, the deep blue bays and curving shoreline offer an inviting resting place for the many pleasure craft that visit the island.

During the War of 1812, the waters west of South Bass Island were the site of a fierce battle between British naval vessels and the newly launched American fleet. On September 10, 1813, the young U.S. Commander Oliver Hazard Perry triumphed in a crushing defeat of the British, under the command of Captain Robert Barclay. Perry then wrote to General William H. Harrison the well-known words, "We have met the enemy, and they are ours. ..."

A century later a monument to Perry's victory was erected, but as more than a simple self-congratulatory statue to the victors. It also celebrated the lasting peace and friendship between the United States and Canada, who share the largest unprotected border — 4,000 miles — in the world.

The monument was dedicated on the 100th anniversary of the battle. During the ceremonies the bodies of three British officers and three American officers killed during the fighting were interred beneath the memorial's floor as symbols of brotherhood between the two countries.

In addition to this spectacular monument, South Bass Island also offers an assortment of other activities. Nautical enthusiasts, for instance, will want to visit the Put-In-Bay Historical Society, near the police station on the west side of town. Inside their marine museum is a fresnel lens and a gift shop. You can explore the interior of the island, past stately homes and vineyards, on a rented golf cart or bicycle. You can also tour a cave or browse through the gift shops. Or you can relax in shady De Rivera Park and do little more than watch boats maneuver into the harbor nearby.

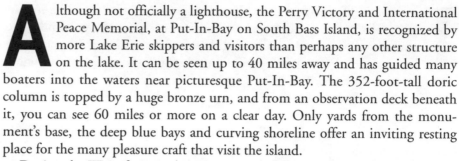

DIRECTIONS: To get to the Miller Boat Line Dock, from O-2 east of Port Clinton, exit onto O-53 north and go approximately 6.2 miles to the highway's end at Catawba Island.

Once on South Bass Island, for a small charge you can take a tram from the ferry dock two miles to Put-In-Bay. The dropoff point is at the corner of Toledo Ave. and Delaware in downtown Put-In-Bay. To get to Perry's monument, follow Delaware one block east.

NOTE: Vehicles may also be transported to South Bass Island on the Miller Boat Line. Reservations are recommended. Contact Miller Boat Line Inc., Route 53 N., Port Clinton, OH 43452; (419) 285-2421. We have found, however, that it is more convenient and fun to explore the island using rental bicycles and golf carts. And, on weekends to avoid congestion in the downtown area of Put-In-Bay, vehicles are not allowed to make a one-day round trip.

Marblehead Lighthouse

Marblehead Lighthouse, the oldest continuously operating light on the Great Lakes, is located on the northeastern tip of beautiful Marblehead Peninsula. Marking the northern boundary of Sandusky Bay, the peninsula itself is surrounded by several islands, each with its own unique history. Just to the south, Johnson's Island (which has a connecting bridge) was once the unpleasant destination for Confederate officer prisoners of war. Today you can visit the site of the camp and walk in the footsteps of those

"During an era when for most females the only 'respectable' choice for career was wife and mother, these women showed the courage of true pioneers."

"During the wildest storms, waves crash against the stone shoreline beneath the light, sending spray nearly the entire 65-foot height of the dripping tower."

long-ago men.

Kelley's Island, just three miles north of Marblehead Peninsula, is another popular destination. Visitors take car ferries from the peninsula to the island, where they explore a rich collection of glacial rock formations and petroglyphs created by the now-extinct Erie Indians.

The area surrounding Marblehead Peninsula and extending through nearby Ottawa, Sandusky, Seneca, and Huron counties is known as the Lake Erie Firelands. Families in Connecticut who had been burned off their lands by the British during the Revolutionary War were given a portion of the 500,000 acres as recompense for their loss.

The first light here was built in 1821 and was called the Sandusky Bay Lighthouse until 1870, when the name was changed to Marblehead. Benajah Wolcott, a veteran of the Revolutionary War, was appointed its first keeper, and when he died of cholera 10 years later, his wife Rachel took on the responsibilities of running the light. The pattern was repeated 64 years later when, in 1896, head keeper George McGee died and was succeeded by his wife. During an era when for most females the only "respectable" choice for career was wife and mother, these women showed the courage of true pioneers.

One of the reasons the light at Marblehead was built was because of the fierce storms that can blow up in the area, one of the roughest sections of Lake Erie. A northeaster, which has clear passage from Buffalo to Marblehead (nearly 200 miles), can stir the lake into a frenzy. During the wildest storms, waves crash against the stone shoreline beneath the light, sending spray nearly the entire 65-foot height of the dripping tower.

Storms also took a heavy toll on ships in the area. Many foundered and several sank, and for more than 50 years, crews stationed at the lighthouse had the dangerous responsibility of attempting rescues. Finally, in 1876 a separate life saving station was established in the area.

Between 1897 and 1903, the tower was extended 15 feet to its current height of 65 feet, and a new lantern was installed. In 1923 the light was converted to electric power, and the 1946 shipping season saw the last keeper at Marblehead.

Today, the light still guards the waters off the peninsula, guiding ships in and out of Sandusky Bay. Bordered by trees along the shoreline, the round limestone tower narrows as it rises to the bright red metal railing surrounding the walkway. A matching red roof and ventilator ball caps a 10-sided lantern room that encloses a green beacon. The beautiful fresnel lens installed in 1903 is on exhibit at the Coast Guard Station near the light.

The keeper's house, divided from the light tower by a tall row of fragrant cedars, was ordered burned by the Coast Guard in 1969 because of extensive damage by vandals. It was saved, however, by a local citizen's protest and is now under the protection of the Ohio DNR, which uses it as a residence.

The light tower is open for tours the second Saturday of June, July, August and September. For group tours write the U.S. Coast Guard Station, Marblehead, Ohio 43440.

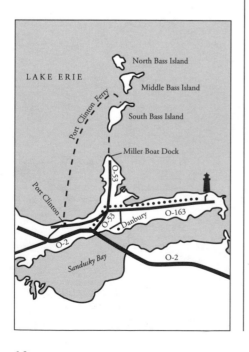

DIRECTIONS: From O-2 east of Port Clinton, exit onto O-53 and go north 1.2 miles to O-163. Turn right (east) onto O-163 and go approximately 8.1 miles to Lighthouse Dr., just past the entrance to St. Mary Byzantine Catholic Church in Marblehead. Turn left (north) onto Lighthouse Dr. and go about 0.1 mile.

Sandusky Harbor Pierhead Light

The light that guides boats into Sandusky Harbor sits on a long, rough stone pier that juts out into the blue-green waters of Lake Erie. The rusty, 20-foot-tall skeleton rests on a thick concrete foundation and supports a small, square room surrounded by a narrow walkway. The only way to see this light is from the water, and it's an interesting perspective. On the mainland shore behind the light, waves of metal and wood tracks rise above the treeline and plunge out of sight, a dizzying display of rollercoasters at the Cedar Point Amusement Park.

"Behind the light, waves of metal and wood tracks rise above the treeline and plunge out of sight."

Huron Harbor Pierhead Light

"The park — with a playground, picnic area and swimming beach — is an ideal location to view the white steel light."

The Huron Harbor Pierhead Light is at the end of a long concrete pier across the river from Nickleplate Park. Stretching along the Lake Erie shore, the park — with a playground, picnic area, and swimming beach — is an ideal location to view the white steel light. From its square base, the light curves inward and narrows to support the small beacon that guides ships into the harbor.

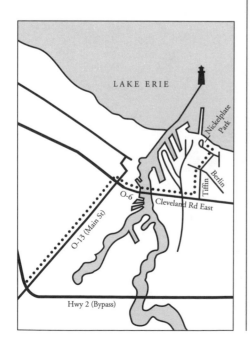

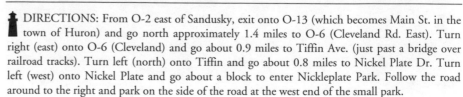

DIRECTIONS: From O-2 east of Sandusky, exit onto O-13 (which becomes Main St. in the town of Huron) and go north approximately 1.4 miles to O-6 (Cleveland Rd. East). Turn right (east) onto O-6 (Cleveland) and go about 0.9 miles to Tiffin Ave. (just past a bridge over railroad tracks). Turn left (north) onto Tiffin and go about 0.8 miles to Nickel Plate Dr. Turn left (west) onto Nickel Plate and go about a block to enter Nickleplate Park. Follow the road around to the right and park on the side of the road at the west end of the small park.

Vermilion Lighthouse Replica

Originally built in 1877 at the end of a wooden pier, the Vermilion Lighthouse was the symbol of the entire port town and its way of life. Vermilion was once known as the "city of sea captains" and for good reason. At one time more than a hundred ships' captains called the town home.

Lighthouses have always fascinated curious children, and the Vermilion light was no different. Young boys dared each other to walk around the outside of the light, across the narrow cement foundation high above the water. They even discovered a secret entrance — through a hole in the foundation and then through a manhole cover on the first floor of the interior of the light.

Ted Wakefield, who was born and raised in Vermilion, was one of those young boys, and he considered the light the most important landmark around. Each day during his childhood, Ted's gaze moved across the water to the light-

"He never allowed his memory of the lighthouse to fade, and his deep love for it permeated his life."

"The lighthouse appeared to be on the verge of collapse, teetering dangerously close to the side of the pier."

house as a matter of habit.

One morning in 1929, his eyes detected what no one else's had — the lighthouse appeared to be on the verge of collapse, teetering dangerously close to the side of the pier. Ted informed his father, and he in turn reported the situation to the Lighthouse Service. But instead of repairing the light, as Ted had hoped, service workers tore it down with surprising quickness.

The feeling of having something precious stolen from him remained with Ted as he grew to adulthood. He never allowed his memory of the lighthouse to fade, and his deep love for it permeated his life. Not suprisingly then, during the 1980s Ted led a campaign that raised $55,000, to rebuild the light in exactly the same way as the original. During the 1991 relighting ceremony, the town of Vermilion acknowledged with pride the dreams and deeds of Ted Wakefield, the native son who had given them back their beloved light.

The reconstructed light now fronts the Inland Seas Maritime Museum, on the lakeshore. Its octagonal base is banded with red-brown, and the rest of the tower is white, with a few small portholes dotting its sides. Near the top a decorative shelf encircles the tower, curving outward gracefully to support the octagonal parapet and black, railed walkway. The lantern room is also black and, as in the original, a fresnel lens graces its interior.

A large propeller rests on the lawn nearby, not far from the museum, which holds one of the best nautical collections we have seen on the Great Lakes. Inside, two floors are devoted to the "sweetwater seas," and a wide range of exhibits includes topographical maps, ship models, china, Lyle Guns, original artwork, fresnel lenses, and even the pilot house from the ship *Canopus*. The Great Lakes Historical Society also maintains a research library on the premises, with files on nearly every Great Lakes subject imaginable. A gift shop features regional books and nautical collectibles.

Membership in the society is open to all interested persons. For information, contact The Great Lakes Historical Society, 480 Main St., Vermilion, OH 44089-1099; (216) 967-3467.

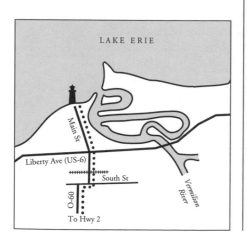

DIRECTIONS: From O-2 between Huron and Lorain, exit onto O-60 (Savannah-Vermilion Rd.) and go north about 1.4 miles to South St. Turn right (east) onto South St. and go 0.1 miles to Main St. Turn left (north) onto Main and go approximately 0.2 miles to Liberty Ave. (US-6). Continue straight ahead (north) on Main three blocks to the Inland Seas Maritime Museum, on the left. The lighthouse is at the north end of the museum building.

Lorain West Breakwater Lighthouse

Fondly called "Jewel of the Port" by locals, the Lorain West Breakwater Light has quietly guarded the harbor of Lorain, Ohio, for more than 75 years. Built in 1917 by the Army Corps of Engineers, the lighthouse rests on a square concrete foundation at the end of a rough stone breakwater. A 4-foot-high, heavy steel railing surrounds the white concrete structure, and small ground-floor windows peer across the platform. A set of rust-colored steps reaches down to the water, and a matching stairway climbs to the front door. Rows of green-shuttered windows encircle the two-story house.

Above the second floor, the red-shingled roof is interrupted by the square light tower, with its own matching green-shuttered window. The tower extends up only one additional story, and the walkway that surrounds the parapet barely rises above the roofline of the house. A steel railing anchored by four thick, white corner posts surrounds the walkway. The round lantern room, with diamond-shaped panes, is topped by a smooth, round metal roof and ventilator ball, both painted red to match the shingles on the house roof just below. A boom extends from above the door of the structure out over the water, still ready to assist in the unloading of supplies necessary to operate a busy light station.

But those days are long past, and the light has stood empty for nearly 30 years. That it is standing at all is a monument to the determination and love the residents of Lorain had for their "Jewel of the Port." When a new automated light was built in 1965, the Coast Guard planned to demolish the old light. But a concerted effort on the part of a quickly organized "save the lighthouse" committee, along with help from Mother Nature, changed the outcome. October storms postponed the demolition, giving the committee time to reach an agreement with the Coast Guard. A local group was given responsibility for the lighthouse for a period of five years, thus saving it from tragic demolition.

After changing ownership a few more times, the lighthouse is now in the caring hands of the Port of Lorain Foundation (City Hall, Room 511, 200 West Erie Avenue, Lorain, Ohio 44052), an energetic nonprofit group whose priority remains the restoration of the light. Plans also include creating a museum inside the light.

" That this light is standing at all is a monument to the determination and love the residents of Lorain had for their Jewel of the Port."

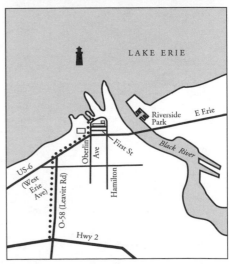

🕯 DIRECTIONS: From O-2 south of Lorain, exit onto O-58 (Leavitt Rd.) and go north approximately 3.1 miles to US-6 (W. Erie Ave). Turn right (east) onto US-6 and go about 1.1 miles to Oberlin Ave. (Look for a Muni Pier Hot Water sign, on the left just before the intersection.) Turn left (north) onto Oberlin and go two blocks (past the old Water Distribution Plant) to First St. Continue straight ahead, across First St., and drive along the left side of the Lorain Water Treatment Plant. Behind that building is a parking area, at the municipal pier. Drive to the end of the parking area and look for the lighthouse in the harbor on the right.

Cleveland West Pierhead Light

Cleveland's beautiful waterfront, with its green parks and towering buildings provides an impressive backdrop to its pierhead lights. Cleveland's West Pierhead Light was home base to a lightkeeper and two assistants during the late 1800s. They were responsible for several lights in the area plus a "cow," a large steam whistle so named because of the deep mooing sound it made with the help of large reflectors positioned behind. With its 12-mile range, the "cow" outdistanced the range of the light by two miles.

One of Cleveland's most illustrious keepers was Captain Fred T. Hatch, who arrived at the station in 1885. Five years later, as keepers around the Great Lakes were often called upon to do, he risked his life in an attempt to save others. During high winds in October 1890, the barge *Wahnapitae* struck the breakwater that connects the East Pierhead and East Entrance lights and began breaking up. Captain Hatch, who had previously been awarded the U.S. Medal of Honor for livesaving, set out in his small, wooden rowboat to attempt a rescue. But by the time he reached the *Wahnapitae*, all hands had been washed overboard and drowned except Catherine Hazen, the barge captain's wife. As Hatch approached, Hazen too was swept into the water, but Hatch was able to pull her into his boat.

Before Hatch could row to safety, however, his boat was swamped and he had to pull Hazen while swimming to the breakwall, where both were pulled out of the water by onlookers. For his courageous rescue, Captain Hatch became the distinguished recipient of a rare honor — a second service bar above his original medal of honor.

Today, the West Pierhead Light still stands at the end of the stone pier whose blocks of rock are now worn smooth and are crumbling in places. Along with the East Pierhead Light, about a half mile away, it marks the entrance to the inner harbor and the Cuyahoga River. The tower and an attached square, white one-story building rest atop a thick concrete foundation. The round, white tower rises 30 feet to its parapet, and small portholes peer out beneath a walkway and railing that surrounds a much narrower, one-story section. That small room supports the lantern, which is surrounded by its own walkway and is enclosed with diamond-shaped panes. The green lantern matches the trim of the doors and windows of both tower and house. The brick-red roofs on both provide an interesting contrast to the muted browns and grays of the city behind.

DIRECTIONS and map, page 19.

CLEVELAND WEST PIERHEAD LIGHT

CLEVELAND EAST AND WEST PIERHEAD LIGHTS

Cleveland East Pierhead Light

"From its pilot house you get a uniquely beautiful view of the Cleveland skyline."

The Cleveland East Pierhead Light perches at the west end of a 4-mile-long breakwall that protects the Cleveland shoreline. It is smaller than the West Pierhead Light, with no attached house, but it also stands about 30 feet tall. A steel wall protects one side of the foundation, and huge, smooth boulders surround the rest of the platform.

A doorway opens at the base of the white tower, and round windows peer out from the top. Above those small openings, a walkway surrounds the black lantern room, and crosshatched panes enclosed the still-shining beacon.

The Cleveland waterfront offers two other nautical attractions, both operated by the Great Lakes Historical Society. One is the steamer *William G. Mather*, which has been turned into a floating museum permanently moored at the East 9th Street Pier. You can explore the vast cargo hold, crew's quarters, dining room and other areas of this former Cleveland Cliffs Iron Company flagship. And from its pilot house you get a uniquely beautiful view of the Cleveland skyline. At an adjacent pier is a second floating museum — the *U.S.S. Cod*, a WWII submarine that provides a fascinating glimpse into the day-to-day lives of the sailors once stationed aboard.

The *Mather* and *Cod* are both open daily from Memorial Day through Labor Day, Monday through Saturday, 10 a.m. to 5 p.m., and Sunday, noon to 5 p.m. In May, September and October, hours are Saturday, 10 a.m. to 5 p.m., and Sunday, noon to 5 p.m. For more information call (216) 574-6262.

Cleveland East Entrance Light

The Cleveland East Harbor Entrance Light is a small skeleton tower at the end of a rocky pier. A square, enclosed room sits atop the white tower, and above that room, a red beacon shines over the waters of Lake Erie, guiding ships into this busy port.

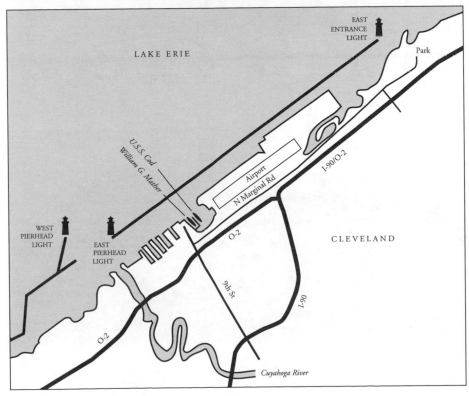

DIRECTIONS: *Cleveland Pierhead Lights:* On I-90 coming from the east, near downtown Cleveland where I-90 makes a sharp curve left (and the speed limit drops to 35 mph), get into the right lanes and exit (straight ahead) onto O-2. Go west on O-2 about a mile to the East 9th St. exit. Go right (north) on E. 9th about two blocks to its end near a parking area by the *William G. Mather* museum ship. The pierhead lights are out in the harbor, to the left. For closer views, board the cruise ship *Goodtime 111*, which departs from near the *Mather*. Phone (216) 861-5110 for more information.

From I-90 coming from the west, exit at East 9th St. and go north approximately 1.5 miles to its end at the museum ship parking lot.

Cleveland East Entrance Light: From the museum ship area, go south on E. 9th St. to N. Marginal Rd. (just past the U.S. Coast Guard Station and just before crossing O-2). Turn left (east) onto N. Marginal and go about 2.7 miles to a stop sign. Bear left, continuing on N. Marginal another 0.4 miles to its end at a public park. The East Entrance Light is at the end of the breakwall.

Fairport Harbor West Breakwater Lighthouse

"Swimmers flock to the beautiful, sandy beach nearby, and the surrounding waters are a favorite of fishermen."

The Fairport Harbor Breakwater Lighthouse has guided ships into Fairport Harbor since 1925. The white two-story structure dominates the end of the dark, rocky breakwater that juts into the harbor. Swimmers flock to the beautiful, sandy beach nearby, and the surrounding waters are a favorite of fishermen.

A flight of steps leads up from the light's thick concrete foundation past the ground level, painted black, to the entry on the first floor. The square tower stretches just above the peak of the house's reddish-brown sheet-metal roof. A square parapet and railing sit atop a small, windowed room in the tower. The lantern room is round and is capped by a roof and ventilator ball, both painted red to match the roof of the house below.

DIRECTIONS and map, page 22.

Old Fairport Harbor Main Lighthouse

In 1825 the first lighthouse was built on the shores of Fairport Harbor, and it became one of the guideposts to the unsettled wilderness area of northern Ohio know as the Western Reserve. Two decades later, as one of the northern "stations" on the Underground Railroad, the light was used by escaped slaves as a refuge and a crossing point to Canada and safety.

By the end of the Civil War, too much settling had damaged the tower, and a new structure was deemed necessary. Constructed on a low rise near shore, the new lighthouse became the dominant landmark in the small town of Fairport. When the structure, including a new keeper's house, was completed in 1871, Joseph Babcock moved in as head keeper and remained in that position for 45 years. Joseph's son Dan was born in the lighthouse and later helped his father with the light station tasks. Eventually Dan Babcock became the light's assistant keeper and then head keeper.

In 1925 a new light and foghorn station were built on the breakwater in the harbor, and it became the keeper's daily responsibility to take a boat out to service the light, a nerve-wracking experience for the keeper's family when they watched during rough seas.

Also when the new breakwater light was built, the old tower on shore became obsolete. The Coast Guard planned to use the dwelling to house their personnel but raze the darkened tower. A determined letter-writing campaign by concerned citizens in the Fairport area, however, convinced the U.S. Secretary of Commerce to reconsider. He let the light stand. The far-sighted

> *"The light was used by escaped slaves as a refuge and a crossing point to Canada and safety."*

OLD FAIRPORT HARBOR MAIN

JOHN FEDAK, FAIRPORT HARBOR HISTORICAL SOCIETY TRUSTEE, IN THE *FRONTENAC* PILOT HOUSE

21

residents of Fairport Harbor had saved a beautiful national treasure, now known as Old Fairport Harbor Main. In 1945 ownership passed from the Coast Guard to the town.

The red-brick two-story keeper's dwelling, trimmed in white, features narrow, arched windows and a square front entrance that extends out from the house. A short, covered passageway runs from the dwelling to the base of the tower. Constructed of Berea sandstone, the tower narrows slightly as it rises, and its gray-brown walls are interrupted by just one small window halfway up. Four arched windows peek out beneath the parapet, which is encircled by an iron fence. A small room, with a small door and a few round windows, supports the 10-sided lantern room, which is topped by a curved steel roof and gold ventilator ball. The beacon is now dim, but it has avoided the painful fate of having its lens destroyed or lost. It is on display below, in the keeper's house.

Today, Old Fairport Harbor Main is a one-of-a-kind lighthouse/maritime museum that includes hundreds of beautiful historical nautical displays, both inside the keeper's house and outside on the lawn. Included are replicas of ships, marine charts, a Lyle Gun and breeches buoy, and the metal ship's mast (now used as a flagpole) from the *U.S.S. Michigan,* the first iron-hulled ship in the U.S. Navy to sail the Great Lakes. Also on display is the Fairport Harbor Range Light, a white 20-foot-tall steel tower with a small platform and light at the top.

One of the most fascinating exhibits is the complete, intact pilot house from the steamer *Frontenac,* which is attached to the west side of the dwelling. You can walk into the pilot house, with its gleaming hardwood walls and wide bank of windows, and wonder or imagine what sights have moved by, what storms have pressed the panes? And we couldn't help but wonder what thoughts passed through the pilot's mind on the ill-fated day when the *Frontenac* swung wide coming out of the Buffalo River and crashed into the breakwater light there with such force that it pushed the light backward 20 feet. (See photo, p. 37).

The museum is open 1 p.m. to 6 p.m. on Wednesdays, Saturdays, Sundays and legal holidays from the Saturday before Memorial Day through Labor Day. For further information or to arrange a group tour call (216) 354-4825.

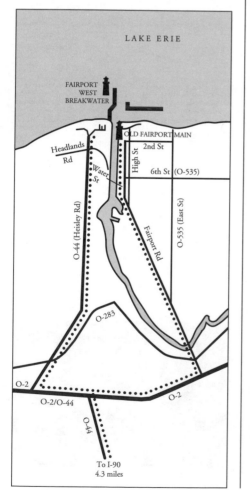

DIRECTIONS: From I-90 approximately 27 miles east of Cleveland, take exit #200 onto O-44 and go north about 4.3 miles to the junction with O-2.

To get to the Old Fairport Main Lighthouse and Museum, turn right (east) onto O-2 and drive about 1.1 miles to Fairport Rd. (the first exit). Turn left (north) onto Fairport and go about 2.1 miles (past the O-535 junction at 0.6 miles and the junction with Water St. at 1.3 miles) to the lighthouse, on the left at the corner of High and 2nd streets.

To get to the Fairport Harbor West Breakwall Lighthouse, from the easternmost junction of O-2 and O-44, go west on O-2/O-44 for 0.7 miles to the western junction of the two highways. Exit right (north) onto O-44 (Heisley Rd.) and drive about 2.5 miles to Headlands Rd. Continue straight ahead across Headlands into the Headlands Beach State Park. Follow the park road around to the right to the parking area. The lighthouse is on the breakwall, a short walk toward the lake, to the right of the parking area (follow the signs to the fishing area).

Ashtabula Lighthouse

" The two men had to first thaw the door open, then tunnel through the ice to freedom."

The first light to guide ships into Ashtabula Harbor was constructed in 1835. Rebuilt in 1905 and again in 1916 as part of harbor improvements, the third light still sits at the end of the rough stone breakwater that protects the harbor. Supported by a concrete foundation and elevated from the breakwater, the first floor of the structure is surrounded by a metal railing. A red metal roof covers half the first story, while the other half rises to support a second story, also capped by a red metal roof. The parapet and lantern of the light tower rise from the center of the second story.

Lake Erie is the most shallow of the Great Lakes, and that trait can exacerbate already fierce weather that can blow through. For instance, during one winter storm in 1928, two keepers stationed here were imprisoned inside their normally peaceful light while savage winds and towering waves pounded the structure for two days. When the storm finally subsided, the keepers tried to escape, but the lighthouse had become a cocoon of ice up to five feet thick in places. The two men had to first thaw the door open, then tunnel through the ice to freedom.

When you visit here, also stop at the Great Lakes Marine and U.S. Coast Guard Memorial Museum, across the parking lot from where you view the light. The museum occupies what was once the lightkeeper's house, and its rooms are filled with a variety of exhibits including a photographic history of Ashtabula, an extensive collection of ship models, and the pilot house from the steamer *Thomas Walters*. There is even a scale model of a Hulett iron-ore unloading machine and, outside near the museum's parking area, an actual bucket from a Hulett unloader. The museum is open 12 to 6 p.m., Fridays, Saturdays, Sundays and holidays from Memorial Day through the end of October. For group tours call (216) 964-6847.

DIRECTIONS: From I-90 west of Conneaut, exit (#229) onto O-11 and go north about 5.4 miles to its end, at 6th St. (O-531) in Ashtabula. Turn left (west) onto 6th and go approximately 0.6 miles, across a swing bridge (6th St. becomes Bridge St. at that point), to Hulbert St., the second street after crossing the bridge. Turn right (north) onto Hulbert and go up the steep hill to its end at Walnut Blvd. Turn right (east) onto Walnut and go one block to its end. On the right is Point Park and a parking area, with good views of the lighthouse out in the harbor to the left. The Coast Guard and Marine Museum are directly across Walnut Blvd. from the parking area.

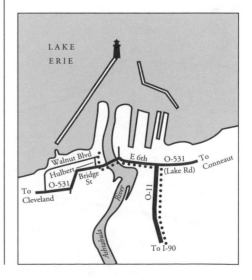

Conneaut West Breakwater Light

" *Nearby is Conneaut Township Park, which offers a beautiful beach, changing rooms and expansive picnic area.* "

The Conneaut West Breakwater Light perches at the end of a rough stone breakwater. A railing surrounds the smooth concrete foundation, and at the center of that base, a second, smaller but taller concrete platform, also surrounded by a fence, rises up to support the lighthouse. The metal light begins as a square first story, then rapidly narrows and continues up as a thin shaft. The white tower is bisected by a thick, black band. Small, round windows dot the structure, and a small railing borders the mechanical light at the top.

The best view of the light comes from the parking area for the public dock and boat ramp, just south of the light. Nearby is Conneaut Township Park, which offers a beautiful beach, changing rooms and expansive picnic area.

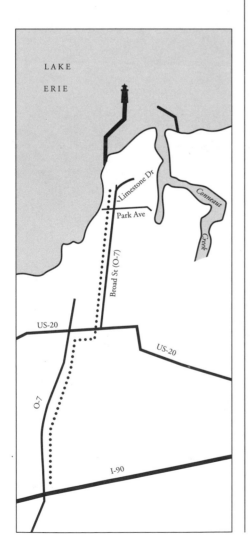

DIRECTIONS: From I-90 exit (#241) onto O-7 and go north 1.8 miles to the junction with US-20, in Conneaut. Turn right (east) onto US-20/O-7 (State Route 20) and go 0.3 miles to Broad St. (O-7). Turn left (north) onto Broad and go approximately 1.6 miles to its end at Park Ave. Continue across Park onto Limestone Dr. to the parking areas for the public dock and boat ramp, which are just south of the light.

Erie Land Lighthouse

Although some sources say the Erie Land Light was put into service in 1813, the U.S. Government listed it as first being lit in 1818, sharing honors with Buffalo as the first lights on Lake Erie. By 1857 the first tower had sunk so much that it had to be torn down and a new one built. The second tower lasted only eight years before it too had to be taken down because of sinking. A conscientious engineer finally took borings of the area, which revealed a layer of quicksand far below. The riddle of the sinking towers solved, adjustments were made and a third tower was built in 1867. Except for closing briefly in the 1880s, it remained in operation until 1899. In 1901 its fresnel lens was moved to Marblehead Lighthouse.

The round, buff-colored stone tower narrows slightly as it rises, and just below the parapet, four small arched windows peek out. A door from a small, round room that supports the lantern room opens to a walkway encircled by a metal railing. A second, smaller railing surrounds the 10-sided lantern room. A small brick building is attached at the base of the tower, and closely trimmed shrubbery borders both of those structures as well as the nearby keeper's house, a square, two-story brick dwelling trimmed in brown.

"The Erie Land Light shares honors with Buffalo as the first lights on Lake Erie."

DIRECTIONS: From the I-90/I-79 interchange, go north on I-79 approximately 5.5 miles to its end on West 12th St., in Erie. Turn right (east) onto 12th and go about 3.5 miles to East Ave. Turn left (north) onto East Ave. and drive about 0.5 miles to Lake Rd. East (Alt. P-5). Turn right (east) onto Lake Rd. and go approximately 0.3 miles to Lighthouse St. Turn left (north) onto Lighthouse St. and go approximately 0.3 miles to its end. The Erie Land Light is on the left.

When leaving, follow Lighthouse St. around to the right (east) and go one block east to Birch Ct. Turn right (south) onto Birch and follow it 0.3 miles back to Lake Rd.

Presque Isle Lighthouse

" The bright flames of burning natural gas wells were often confused with the lighthouse beacon."

Presque Isle Lighthouse is located in a state park on a beautiful peninsula that hooks out into Lake Erie just north of the city of Erie, Pennsylvania. Indian legend tells of a time when several members of the Erie tribe were caught far from shore in a sudden storm. As their cries were heard by the Great Spirit, He stretched his arm out across the water and curved it protectively around them, stilling the waters and saving their lives. Afterward, a sand bar remained in the place the Great Spirit had touched, the peninsula now called Presque Isle.

The point curves to form Erie's harbor, and it was here that the American fleet was constructed during the War of 1812, under the command of Commodore Perry. While wintering here in 1813-1814, many of Perry's troops were stricken with smallpox, and the dead were buried in a nearby pond, later named Graveyard Pond.

The first light in the area was built in Erie Harbor in 1818, tying it with Buffalo as the first lights on Lake Erie. The light on the Presque Isle peninsula was constructed in 1873, and developments near the growing town of Erie later presented difficulties for mariners off the point. In 1882 the lightkeeper informed authorities that the bright flames of burning natural gas wells near Erie, which could be seen by ships north of the peninsula, were often confused with the lighthouse beacon.

Today, the 1873 lighthouse still adds to the beauty of the north shore. The square, white tower rests on a thick limestone base and is topped by a square, black walkway and black lantern room. The light is still operated by the Coast Guard, but the attached keeper's house has been leased to the state park and is used as the park manager's residence. Overlooking the beautiful turquoise water of Lake Erie, the two-story, red-brick keeper's dwelling makes a one-of-a-kind home.

Although it is a private residence, you can get a beautiful, unobstructed view from outside the small picket fence that surrounds the property.

You can also enjoy over six miles of exquisite beaches, hiking trails, bird watching or cross-country skiing. Turtles use the sandy peninsula for spring nesting, and through the summer months wildflowers dot the landscape. An added plus: there is no entry fee to this or any other Pennsylvania State Park.

DIRECTIONS: From the I-90/I-79 interchange, go north on I-79 approximately 5.5 miles to its end at West 12th St., in Erie. Turn left (west) onto 12th and go approximately 1.1 miles to Peninsula Dr. (P-832). Turn right (north) onto Peninsula Dr. and go about 1.3 miles to the entrance of Presque Isle State Park. Enter the park (there is no fee) and follow the one-way loop road around the 14-mile-long peninsula. You can pick up a detailed map of the area at the park office, on the right a mile after entering.

A half mile farther is what appears to be a lighthouse, in a picnic area on the right. It is not an official lighthouse but only a cover, built in 1906 to protect the park's water shut-off valve. Go approximately 4.6 miles farther, to the intersection with Coast Guard Road. Bear left, continuing on the park loop road about two miles, and look for the light on the lake (right) side of the peninsula. You can park on the roadside and, though the lighthouse is a private residence, view and photograph it from outside the surrounding fence.

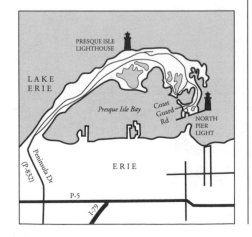

PRESQUE ISLE LIGHTHOUSE

Presque Isle North Pier Light

"In the evening, state park visitors walk along the pier, watching twilight throw shadows and colors across the light."

The Presque Isle North Pier Light is at the end of a short pier that probes the waters of Lake Erie from Presque Isle State Park in Erie, Pennsylvania. The 30-foot-tall, square, white tower is bissected by a black band, and a small, square window peeks out from beneath the parapet. A crosshatched railing secures the walkway, and the black lantern room still houses a light that guides sailors back to shore.

In the evening, state park visitors walk along the pier, gathering driftwood from the gravelly beach and watching twilight throw shadows and colors across the otherwise plain light.

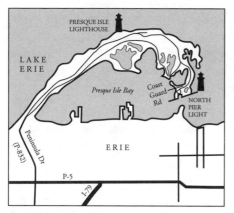

DIRECTIONS: From the I-90/I-79 interchange, go north on I-79 approximately 5.5 miles to its end at West 12th St., in Erie. Turn left (west) onto 12th and go approximately 1.1 miles to Peninsula Dr. (P-832). Turn right (north) onto Peninsula Dr. and go about 1.3 miles to the entrance of Presque Isle State Park. Enter the park (there is no fee) and follow the one-way loop road around the 14-mile-long peninsula. You can pick up a detailed map of the area at the park office, on the right a mile after entering the park.

About a half mile from the park office is what appears to be a lighthouse, in a picnic area on the right. It is not an official lighthouse but only a cover, built in 1906 to protect the park's water shut-off valve. Go approximately 4.6 miles farther, to the intersection with Coast Guard Road.

Turn right (south) onto Coast Guard Road and go about 0.8 miles to the entrance to the Coast Guard Station. As you approach the entrance gate, look for a gravel road on the left. Turn onto that road and follow it a short distance to the parking area at the pier. The light is at the end of the pier.

Barcelona Lighthouse

The Barcelona Light, built in 1828 in response to increased traffic from the newly opened Erie Canal, is a formidable stone tower set on the shore of Barcelona Harbor. The wide, round tower narrows gradually, as its rough, 2-foot-thick walls — made of local beach stones — rise to support the parapet. A dark-brown roof covers a wooden railing that surrounds the unusual lantern — a simple, small glass-enclosed light on a pole.

The Barcelona Light is unique in an even more remarkable way. When the light was built, a pipeline was run up to it from a pocket of natural gas under a nearby creekbed. To the delight of the builder, the innovative system actually worked, making Barcelona the only lighthouse in the world ever to be fueled by its own natural gas deposit and also the first public building in the United States to be fueled by natural gas from any source.

Although the beautiful tower and dwelling are now privately owned, you can get good views from either the highway or the boat launch area next to the light.

> *"The innovative system actually worked, making Barcelona the only lighthouse in the world ever to be fueled by its own natural gas deposit."*

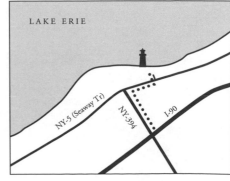

LAKE ERIE

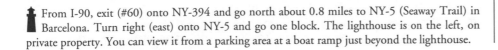

From I-90, exit (#60) onto NY-394 and go north about 0.8 miles to NY-5 (Seaway Trail) in Barcelona. Turn right (east) onto NY-5 and go one block. The lighthouse is on the left, on private property. You can view it from a parking area at a boat ramp just beyond the lighthouse.

Dunkirk Lighthouse Dunkirk Old Tower Light

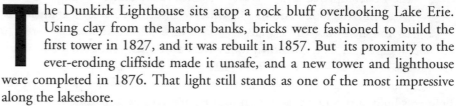

> " *Ornate gargoyle drain spouts at the lantern's roof helped drain off condensation that accumulated on the ceiling of the room when the flame was lit.* "

The Dunkirk Lighthouse sits atop a rock bluff overlooking Lake Erie. Using clay from the harbor banks, bricks were fashioned to build the first tower in 1827, and it was rebuilt in 1857. But its proximity to the ever-eroding cliffside made it unsafe, and a new tower and lighthouse were completed in 1876. That light still stands as one of the most impressive along the lakeshore.

The Victorian-style keeper's dwelling is dark-red brick with a foundation of pale-gray limestone. White-trimmed basement windows peek out from each side of the small front porch, its decorative archway and wooden railing also painted white. The long 12-paned windows of both the first and second story are capped with a heavy limestone lintel. Above each of the three second-story windows is a gable fronted with decorative wooden trim. A delicate wooden spire at the point of each gable reaches skyward, adding a beautiful finishing touch to the house.

A short, enclosed passageway leads from the keeper's dwelling to the square light tower. The first story of the tower is constructed of limestone in a beautiful mixture of dark and light gray. The upper two stories are built of the same stone, but they have been painted white. Marking each level is a small, narrow window that overlooks the lake. At the parapet a square metal railing surrounds the 10-sided lantern. Its base is red, matching its curved metal roof and ventilator ball. Ornate gargoyle drain spouts at the lantern's roof helped drain off condensation that accumulated on the ceiling of the room when the flame was lit.

Not only has this lighthouse and tower been perfectly preserved, it is also the home of the Veteran Park Museum. Inside, individual rooms commemorate each of the five branches of the U.S. armed forces, and a sixth room is dedicated to Vietnam War veterans. A maritime history display is included, and an authentic replica of the lighthouse keeper's kitchen and bedroom give life to bygone days. Construction of new handicapped-accessible restrooms are scheduled for a summer 1994 completion.

And a rare treat: you can climb the lighthouse tower. The black spiral stairway is cast iron, with intricate filigree on each step. From the heights of the tower, you can look into the greenish-blue depths of the lake below. The lawn cuts between the tower and the cliff, and a fence keeps explorers away from the bluff's edge.

Nearby is an old light tower that once stood on the pierhead at the harbor entrance. The white, steel skeleton light has an enclosed first level with a ladder rising up the center of the tower and ending at a small platform that supports the red beacon. One of Buffalo Harbor's Bottle Lights, which take their name

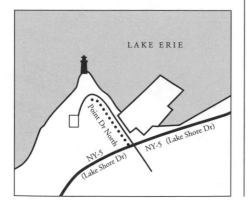

LAKE ERIE

Point Dr North

NY-5 (Lake Shore Dr)

NY-5 (Lake Shore Dr)

DIRECTIONS: From NY-5 (also called Lake Shore Drive and Seaway Trail) near the western edge of Dunkirk, turn north onto Point Drive N. and go 0.5 miles to where it turns left. Look for the lighthouse and parking area directly ahead, on the right side of the road.

from their wine-bottle shape, also sits on the lawn. And a 40-foot-long light-house buoy tender and two rescue boats are among several other maritime arti-facts that dot the grounds.

Museum hours are: April and May, 10 a.m. to 2 p.m., daily except Sundays and Wednesdays; June through August, 10 a.m. to 4 p.m., daily (last tour begins at 3:15 pm.); September through November, 10 a.m. to 3 p.m. (last tour begins at 2:15 p.m.), daily except Sundays and Wednesdays. There is an admis-sion charge for tours.

DUNKIRK LIGHTHOUSE MUSEUM

Sturgeon Point Lighthouse

I n 1924 a developer erected a small lighthouse to mark the entrance to an exclusive private subdivision he had created on a beautiful patch of Lake Erie shoreline known as Sturgeon Point. The lighthouse was later moved to the entrance of a waterworks plant more than a mile inland. Several steps lead up to a blue entry door, which is set inside a protruding stone arch. The circular stone tower rises two stories to a round metal walkway just below the long, narrow glass panes that surround the blue-green octagonal lantern room.

 DIRECTIONS: From NY-5 approximately 6.5 miles south of Wanakah and 1.4 miles north of Evans Center, turn west onto Sturgeon Point Rd. (look for the Jerusalem Corners Elementary School, on the southwest corner of the intersection) and go about 1.1 miles to Old Lakeshore Rd. (Seaway Trail). Turn right (north) onto Old Lakeshore and drive about 0.3 miles to the lighthouse, on the left.

South Buffalo Lighthouse

The South Buffalo Lighthouse is a round, 30-foot-tall steel structure on the end of an industrial pier near the south entrance to the harbor. Its circular base, painted black, rises 10 feet to support a white tower that tapers upward to the parapet and lantern room, glazed with diamond-shaped panes.

This light is on a private pier that is closed to visitors, and the best views come from the water. That may change, however. Plans are underway to dismantle the light and move it to Naval Park in downtown Buffalo.

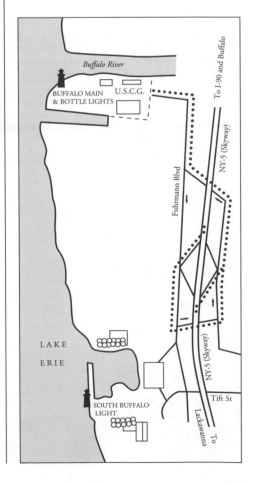

DIRECTIONS: From NY-5 (the Skyway) in downtown Buffalo a little more than a mile south of I-190, take the Fuhrmann Blvd. exit (also marked as the exit to the U.S. Coast Guard Station) and follow the signs to the Coast Guard Station. Exiting the Skyway from the north, go on Fuhrmann (a one-way route south) a few blocks, make a U-turn under the Skyway, and head north on the service road that parallels the freeway. About 0.5 miles farther, jog left, again crossing under the freeway, and take Fuhrmann right (north) approximately 0.6 miles to its end at the U.S. Coast Guard Station.

Exiting the Skyway from the south, follow the service road that parallels the east side of the freeway for about 0.5 miles, jog left, cross under the freeway, and take Fuhrmann right (north) approximately 0.6 miles to its end at the U.S. Coast Guard Station. Park outside the fence and walk toward the river. There is a separate gate that opens into the walking museum alongside the Coast Guard station.

The Old Buffalo Main Lighthouse (p. 34) and one of the old Bottle Lights are behind the Coast Guard buildings. From there you can also see the Horseshoe Reef Light ruins (p. 38) out in the river. (You can also get a good view of the Horseshoe Reef Light ruins from Fort Erie, on the Canadian side of the Niagara River.)

To get to the South Buffalo Light from the Coast Guard Station, take Fuhrmann Blvd. approximately 1.2 miles south to Tift St., and look for the light, on a pier to your right. The light is on private property, but you can get an acceptable view of it from this point.

Old Buffalo Main Lighthouse
Buffalo Bottle Light

"During Prohibition, law enforcement officials used the old tower as a lookout for rum-runners crossing from Canada."

The Buffalo Light, built in 1833 as the area's second beacon, is the oldest structure still standing in its original location in the city of Buffalo. The first light here, a 30-foot-tall stone tower constructed in 1818, was one of the first two lighthouses to grace Lake Erie. (The Erie, Pennsylvania, light was lit the same year.) Three years later the passenger ferry *Walk-In-the-Water* beached near the lighthouse. Though the proximity to the light helped prevent casualties, some blamed the lighthouse for causing the accident. Its beam was not powerful enough, they said, to cut through the sometimes-thick smoke — including the day the *Walk-On-the Water* foundered — from the hundreds of woodburning stoves in the young town of Buffalo.

The debate over the light's effectiveness raged until the opening of the Erie

Canal in 1825, when it it was decided to build a second light. That light, still standing at the Coast Guard station, is a tall, tan stone tower built at the end of a pier. From the beginning, residents were proud of the light, and the city of Buffalo even incorporated it into its city seal. One local man once went so far as to suggest that this light was the most beautiful structure in the world. It does have a graceful beauty that has deepened over the years.

The octagonal tower narrows gradually as it rises, its smooth stone walls interrupted only by a few narrow windows. Directly below the parapet, a bank of set-in windows that encircle the tower are topped by an intricate iron railing. Extending above this rail, a second, smaller and less-ornate walkway surrounds the lantern room. The 10-sided lantern room is entirely glazed, and drainspouts take the form of decorative lion heads at its edges. The roof and ventilator ball have the familiar green color of exposed copper.

The stone tower maintained its vigil from 1833 to 1914, but its importance diminished after a series of lights were built, beginning in 1872, on a breakwater that enlarged the harbor.

The first of those breakwater lights became a magnet for ships, which rammed it in 1899, 1900, 1909 and 1910. The accidents weakened the structure, and in 1914 the breakwater light was rebuilt, using the beacon from the stone tower. The only time the old tower was used again was during Prohibition, when law enforcement officials used it as a lookout for rumrunners crossing from Canada.

After the improvements to the breakwater and its light, it suffered a final assault. In 1958 the freighter *Frontenac*, while making a sweeping turn from the Buffalo River, rammed the breakwater light with such force it knocked it backward 20 feet and gave it a permanent 15-degree tilt (photo, p. 37). Finally in 1961, a skeleton tower was built to support a third, new breakwater light, and the "Leaning Lighthouse" was demolished.

The grounds of the Coast Guard Station here are open to the public seven days a week from 8 a.m. to sunset, and you can walk next to the beautiful, old stone tower as well as a white bottle light nearby. A pair of these lights, named because of their unique shape, were used to mark the entrance to the harbor in the first years of the 20th century.

"The Buffalo Light is the oldest structure still standing in its original location in the city of Buffalo."

DIRECTIONS and map, page 33.

OLD BUFFALO MAIN LIGHTHOUSE

THE BUFFALO "LEANING LIGHTHOUSE." (*Buffalo Evening News* photo courtesy of the Great Lakes Historical Society, Vermilion, Ohio.

Horseshoe Reef Lighthouse Ruins

"Two keepers boated out about a mile to service the light daily."

The Horseshoe Reef Light is an abandoned light at the entrance to the Niagara River from Lake Erie. Its once-strong foundation has crumbled in areas, leaving piles of heavy stone surrounding the base of the light. Four steel legs originally supported a metal platform that held a wooden one-story lighthouse. Today, only the metal shell remains. Its lantern room still retains its shape, and that is the only reminder of the important position this building once held.

So important, in fact, that it needed American, Canadian and British involvement to get built. When a light was originally planned for the area, Horseshoe Reef was deemed unsuitable, since it was too close to shore, and so Middle Reef was chosen as the site. Unfortunately for the Americans, Middle Reef was in Canadian Waters. This set in motion an elaborate network of Canadian and British officialdom discussing and eventually giving permission for the light to be built. Britain ceded the amount of underwater reef necessary for the construction of the light, and on September 1, 1856, the light shone for the first time. Curiously, although standing at Middle Reef, it retained its original name of Horseshoe Reef Light.

The light, with its bare-metal architecture and absence of surrounding land, was not a favorite posting for lightkeepers. Two at a time were appointed, and they lived on shore and boated out about a mile to service the light daily. There were sparse quarters at the light, which were used only in bad weather.

In 1913 the Canadian boundary was moved, and the light became included in American waters. In 1920 — with the advent of the Buffalo Crib Light and a newly created protective channel — this light was abandoned.

DIRECTIONS and map, page 33.

Grand Island Old Front Range Light

T he Old Front Range on Grand Island in the Niagara River, is a beautiful four-story octagonal structure painted brilliant white. Its horizontal wood slats create a pretty pattern interrupted on the first floor only by a door and small window. Above the black-shingled roof of that level, the tower narrows sharply but gracefully as it angles upward. Small windows with slight overhangs dot the tower, and dozens of decorative brackets support the parapet. A black iron rail lines the octagonal walkway, and the white lantern room is surrounded by square windows. A gold-colored ventilator provides a shining cap to this pristine structure.

The light, which is on private property, can best be seen from the river. Its rear range light, a rusty skeleton tower, is also on private property.

Fort Niagara Lighthouse

"The parapet and lantern were placed on the roof of the 'castle,' a large two-story structure with a myriad of uses in the daily life of the fort."

Fort Niagara, at the mouth of the Niagara River, was established by the French in 1726. Because of the natural harbor, this was a favored port for ships traveling Lake Ontario. During the Revolutionary War, lake traffic became heavy enough to warrant a beacon in the area, and in 1781 the first light to shine on the Great Lakes was erected at Fort Niagara.

Instead of building a new tower structure, however, the parapet and lantern were placed on the roof of the "castle," a large two-story structure with a myriad of uses in the daily life of the fort. The beacon shone from that spot until 1803, from when there was no light until a second beacon again sat atop the "castle" from 1822 to 1872.

The light you see today was built in 1872, and in addition to the stone tower, it also once had a small workroom attached to the base. The octagonal tower is constructed of rough, gray cut stone, with a vertical line of beautiful arched windows set into the wall, one in each of four stories. Circling the top of the fourth level is a heavy border of protruding stone that shelters a bank of miniature windows, each with its own matching arch. The original tower ended at that level, but in 1900 its height was extended by the addition of a round room of yellow brick, with its own narrow, arched windows. The lantern room above is surrounded by a black metal railing and is topped by a matching black metal roof and ventilator ball. This lantern shone for more than 120 years before finally being darkened in June 1993, after the completion of a new light nearby.

The attached watch house — its door and windows all matching the arched design of the tower — is currently leased from the Coast Guard by the Old Fort Niagara Association, which maintains exhibits and a museum shop inside.

The lighthouse stands within Old Fort Niagara State Park, and there is a small fee to enter. The park also takes in beautifully spacious grounds, a swimming area, and historic Old Fort Niagara, with its trading post, the "castle," and other original structures integral to the fort's operation.

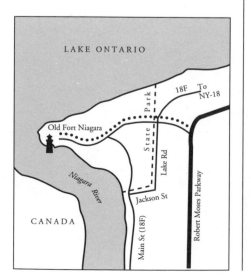

DIRECTIONS: From the south (Niagara Falls area), take the Robert Moses Parkway to Fort Niagara and follow the signs to the Fort Niagara State Park entrance. It is approximately 14 miles from where you get on the Robert Moses Parkway in Niagara Falls to the entrance of Fort Niagara State Park.

From the east, take NY-18 to the Robert Moses Parkway, about 7 miles west of the town of Wilson. Follow the parkway (and signs to Fort Niagara) west approximately 3.2 miles to the state park entrance.

FORT NIAGARA LIGHTHOUSE

Thirty Mile Point Lighthouse

Within the confines of Golden Hill State Park, 30 miles east of the Niagara River mouth, is one of the most beautiful, accessible lighthouses we have visited. Built in 1875, 30 Mile Point Lighthouse warned vessels sailing Lake Ontario of the dangers of nearby shoals and sandbars for more than 75 years, and its beacon could be seen 18 miles offshore. From the slate roof down the dove-gray, hand-cut stone walls to the rough, gray stone basement, the grace and charm of this structure remain strong.

White trim along the narrow 12-paned windows highlights the pale gray of the stone, and peaked gables are supported by decorative arches. The impressive matching gray stone tower is four stories tall. The parapet, surrounded by a white metal railing, supports an enclosed room that, in turn, supports the lantern room.

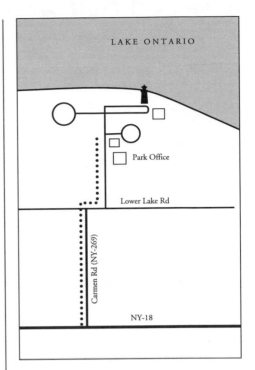

The 10-sided lantern room is glazed with long, rectangular panes, and its metal roof is painted red-orange, a color repeated in a bright strip of trim running along the edge of the roof. A later addition, on the east end of the house, was built of smooth, tan brick atop the original stone basement. Though some attempt was made to blend the roofs, the change in the surface of the building, from gray stone to yellow brick, is quite obvious.

The 30 Mile Point Light was taken out of service in 1958, and in 1984 the Niagara Frontier State Parks Commision signed a lengthy lease for the property. Today, you can tour a museum inside the keeper's dwelling. The tower, too, is open, and a panoramic view of the beautiful park grounds and Lake Ontario beyond awaits those who negotiate the twisting stairs. The grounds surrounding the lighthouse have been turned into campsites, and the foghorn building now houses a recreation room.

DIRECTIONS: From the junction of NY-18 and NY-148 at Somerset, go east on NY-18 about 3 miles to Carmen Rd. (NY-269). (If you are coming from the east on NY-18, this intersection is 1.6 miles west of the first junction with NY-269.)

Turn north onto Carmen and drive about 1.3 miles to Lower Lake Rd. Turn right (east) onto Lower Lake and go about 0.4 miles to Golden Hill State Park. Turn left and follow the entrance road 0.5 miles to the park office, on the right, where you can get a park map. The lighthouse is within sight of the park office.

35

Braddock Point Lighthouse

What was once known as the Braddock Point Lighthouse is now a private residence. Unfortunately, most of the tower is gone, but you can still view the house from the waters off the point.

Charlotte-Genesee Lighthouse

"The small, white enclosed porch must have been a perfect spot to take a break from the arduous tasks of running a lighthouse."

In 1822 Rochester, New York, was a bustling frontier town with an ever-increasing amount of river traffic. As a result, a much-needed lighthouse was built overlooking the mouth of the Genesee River in the small town of Charlotte, just north of Rochester. Through the years a series of piers were also erected to help stop shifting sand bars, which added to the danger of the area. After sand had built up around one pier, a new pier would be erected farther away. This process resulted in the lighthouse becoming a little farther from the water's edge than originally intended.

The keeper's house was rebuilt in 1863, and that two-story red-brick dwelling and original stone tower still stand where lake and river join. A square addition jutting out from the eastern wall of the dwelling is fronted by a small, white enclosed porch that must have been a perfect spot to take a break from the arduous tasks of running a lighthouse.

The tower is constructed of rough-hewn stone, with colors varying from rich chocolate brown to a deep charcoal gray. The octagonal tower narrows slightly to support a rounded black parapet and 10-sided lantern room capped with a

black steel roof and ventilator ball.

Although the light was put out of service in 1881, the dwelling provided a cozy home for lighthouse service personnel until 1940, when the structure was turned over to the Coast Guard. After 20 years of not using the light, the Coast Guard decided to demolish it. That their plans were challenged wasn't too surprising, but by whom may have been. It was local high school students who organized a letter-writing campaign effective enough to reverse the Coast Guard's decision. In 1965 ownership passed into the hands of a newly formed group called the Charlotte-Genesee Lighthouse Historical Society.

But before any visitors could be allowed into the lighthouse, a lengthy and exhaustive renovation was necessary. The entire community pitched in to help with fundraisers and to offer free labor. But the society still faced perhaps their most difficult problem — where to find a lantern room to place atop the bare tower. Fortunately, it presented not a problem, but only a challenge, to local Technical High School students, who built the lantern room that now graces the tower.

In June 1984, during the area's annual Rediscover the River Day celebration, throngs gathered to watch the light, restored to its past grandeur, shine again across Lake Ontario.

You can visit the lighthouse and tower on weekends, when the society opens the dwelling to the public. A museum and gift shop are located inside the keeper's house. The museum is open on Saturdays and Sundays, May through October, from 1 to 5 p.m. For further information or to arrange a group tour call (716) 621-6179.

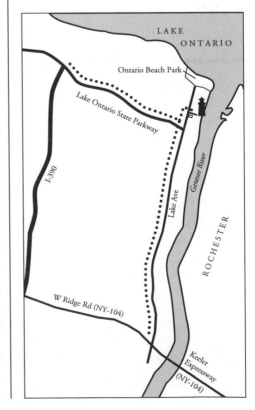

DIRECTIONS: If approaching Rochester from the west, turn north onto I-390 and take the expressway to its end at the Lake Ontario Parkway. Turn right (east) onto the Parkway and go 2.8 miles to its end at Lake Ave. Turn left (north) onto Lake and drive 0.3 miles to the Holy Cross Church. Just past the church building turn right (east). The entrance to the lighthouse area is from the parking lot behind the church.

If coming through Rochester from the east, take the Keeler Expressway (NY-104) west to its end at a traffic signal at Lake Ave., a short distance after the freeway ends. Turn right (north) onto Lake and go approximately 4.2 miles to the Holy Cross Church. Just past the church building turn right (east). The entrance to the lighthouse area is from the parking lot behind the church.

Sodus Point Lighthouse

"A park surrounding the light has plenty of picnic tables. Inviting lawns stretch toward the lake, and wild roses dot the shoreline. "

The first light at Sodus Bay was put into service in 1825, but by 1871 it was in such a state of disrepair that a new light was built. The beacon from that beautiful gray limestone light shone across the waters of Lake Ontario for only 30 years before it too was darkened, but not abandoned or destroyed. By 1901 a new light was built on the end of a pier marking the new entrance to Sodus Bay, and the lightkeeper responsible for servicing it was stationed in the old lighthouse. Today you can tour the beautiful lighthouse, now maintained by the Sodus Bay Historical Society, which leased it in 1984.

The cut-stone exterior gives the light a rugged look, and its attached tower is a sturdy square rising nearly 50 feet, with square four-paned windows marking each of the three levels. The black parapet and lantern room guard a light that has been dark for more than 90 years. To the rear of the building, a white two-story wooden house has been added, with a covered front porch and flower boxes that give it a country charm.

Inside is a marine museum that is open daily from May 1 to October 31, 10 a.m. to 5 p.m. A park surrounding the light has plenty of picnic tables plus a pavilion for large gatherings. Inviting lawns stretch toward the lake, and wild roses dot the shoreline. During the summer months, the historical society also sponsors an outdoor concert series here.

Sodus Outer Light

Built in 1903 at the end of a long, narrow pier, the 45-foot-tall Sodus Outer Light (also known as the Sodus Bay Pierhead Light) replaced the Big Sodus Light, on the bluff nearby, and made it obsolete. Today, the pierhead light's square, white tower and red lantern is the first sight to greet skippers visiting Sodus Bay.

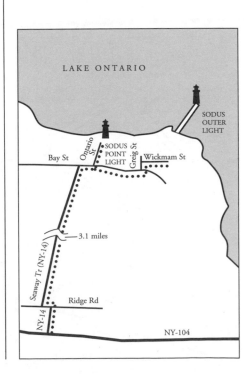

DIRECTIONS: From NY-104 about midway between Rochester and Oswego, turn north onto NY-14 and go 0.3 miles to Ridge Rd. Turn left (west) onto Ridge and go 0.1 mile to Seaway Trail ((NY-14). Turn right (north) onto Seaway and drive about 3.1 miles to Bay St. Turn right (east) onto Bay and go one block to Ontario St. Turn left (north) onto Ontario and go 0.2 miles to its end at the parking area for the Sodus Lighthouse Museum.

You can view the Sodus Outer Light from the lighthouse grounds or get a closer look as follows. Return to Bay Street, turn left (east) and go about two blocks to Greig St., on the left (a gas station/party store is on the left at this intersection). Turn left (north) onto Greig and go one block to Wickham St. Turn right (east) onto Wickham and follow it to its end at the parking area. You can walk out to the outer light.

Oswego West Pierhead Lighthouse

" Unique hands-on areas are favorites of young children, who can touch and feel history."

Because of Oswego's strategic location at the eastern tip of Lake Ontario, a light has stood watch over this area since 1834. The most recent lighthouse, the Oswego West Pierhead Light, was built in 1930. It sits atop a square concrete foundation 10 feet above the water's touch, and that base curves out gracefully to support a metal railing surrounding the light. The red roofline of the small, white, square house resting at the center of the platform is interrupted only by a thin, white chimney. The square light tower rises about 15 feet above the center peak of the house, ending with a black iron walkway and white lantern room. Its red cap and ventilator ball match the red roof below, and its light still shines over the waters of Oswego. Two narrow, red-and-white skeleton towers have been added to the pierhead to assist in navigation.

On the waterfront nearby is the H. Lee White museum, with local-history exhibits that range from the days of the Iroquois Indians three centuries ago, through Colonial America, to the present. Unique hands-on areas are favorites of young children, who can touch and feel history. Two exhibits — the LT-5 *Nast*, a large tug from the Normandy Invasion Fleet, and the *Lance Knapp*, a steam-powered derrick barge — float in the water adjacent to the museum building. The museum is open to the public from Memorial Day to Labor Day and year-round by appointment. Hours are June weekends, 10 a.m. to 5 p.m., and July and August, daily, 10 a.m. to 5 p.m. Admission is free.

Also in Oswego is the beautiful Fort Ontario State Historic Site overlooking Lake Ontario. All buildings are authentic, and during the summer, daily drills and ceremonies are peformed.

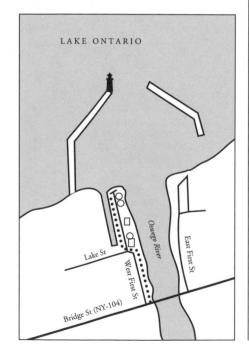

LAKE ONTARIO

Oswego River

Lake St

West First St

East First St

Bridge St (NY-104)

⚓ DIRECTIONS: From NY-104 (Bridge St.) just west of the Oswego River in Oswego, turn north onto West First St. and go (toward the large grain elevators in front of you) about four blocks to Lake St. Continue following West First St. as it crosses Lake, jogs slightly left, cuts through a fence, skirts left of the grain elevators, passes by the H. Lee White Marine Museum Annex (a barge on the left), to the the H. Lee White Marine Museum, on the right. Total distance from where you turn onto West First is 0.6 miles.

Though visitors are not allowed on the lighthouse pier itself, you can get good views from the end of a pier that extends out from the museum.

Selkirk Lighthouse

The Selkirk Lighthouse — erected in 1838 at the mouth of the Salmon River, four miles west of Pulaski and decommissioned in 1859 — has continued guarding those shores for more than 155 years. Built into the side of a hill, the lighthouse has a walkout basement with a single, small six-paned window and a wide, weather-beaten wood door. The dwelling is made of beautiful chocolate-colored stones with bright patches of gray stone and mortar marking spots where repairs have been made in more recent years. Square windows are set into the walls at regular intervals, and a white addition has been built at the rear of the house. A large guardrail protects a corner of the house that is less than a yard from a road curving abruptly between it and the shoreline.

The light tower, covered in dark wood shingles, rises from the front peak of the house's metal-sheathed roof. There is just enough room for a small white-trimmed window to peek out beneath the octagonal parapet. A round railing surrounds the lantern, and other rails run vertically from it to curve over to the top of the lantern room, resulting in a playground jungle-gym look. Each of the lantern room's eight sides is covered floor to ceiling with a beautiful pattern composed of more than a dozen small glass panes.

> *"A corner of the house is less than a yard from a road that curves abruptly between it and the shoreline."*

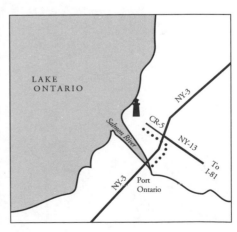

DIRECTIONS: From the village of Port Ontario, travel north on NY-3 approximately 0.2 miles to County Road 5 (just across the Salmon River and marked by a blinker light). Turn left (west) onto CR-5 and go about 0.8 miles to the lighthouse, on the right, near the end of the road. This is a very congested area with little parking available.

Stony Point Lighthouse

"It stands today much as it did the first day it shined across its Lake Ontario waters."

The Stony Point Lighthouse, southwest of Sackets Harbor, was built in 1837. Although it was refitted in 1857, it stands today much as it did when it first shined across its Lake Ontario waters. The white, 60-foot-high tower is made of brick, with decorative arches and rounded corners worked into its surface. The square tower widens slightly to support the now-empty, black parapet and lantern room. The large two-story keeper's house is attached to the base of the tower, and dormer windows poke out from its roofline. A beautiful expanse of lawn stretches from the structure to the rocky shoreline of the lake, which fills the horizon with blue swells.

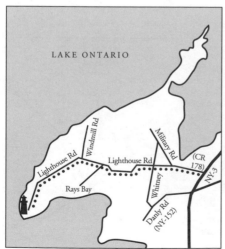

LAKE ONTARIO

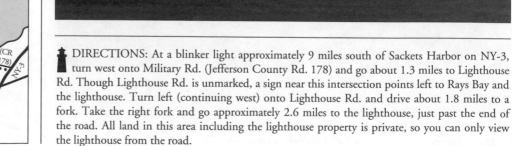

DIRECTIONS: At a blinker light approximately 9 miles south of Sackets Harbor on NY-3, turn west onto Military Rd. (Jefferson County Rd. 178) and go about 1.3 miles to Lighthouse Rd. Though Lighthouse Rd. is unmarked, a sign near this intersection points left to Rays Bay and the lighthouse. Turn left (continuing west) onto Lighthouse Rd. and drive about 1.8 miles to a fork. Take the right fork and go approximately 2.6 miles to the lighthouse, just past the end of the road. All land in this area including the lighthouse property is private, so you can only view the lighthouse from the road.

Galloo Island Lighthouse

The Galloo Island Lighthouse sits on a remote stretch of gray, rocky shoreline overlooking Lake Ontario 16 miles west of Sackets Harbor. The first light was built here in 1820 to help warn mariners of shoals near the island. During reconstruction in 1867, the tower was shortened 11 feet.

Lush greenery surrounding this long-abandoned station gives it a wild air. The stone keeper's house is still intact, but a wooden addition on its side has greatly deteriorated. Windows and doors have been boarded up, but at the same time a few missing boards in the walls leave dark, exposed gaps.

A short, enclosed walkway joins the house to the 50-foot-tall tower. Long, narrow gray stones make up the circular tower, with a few small, square windows interrupting the row upon row of stone. The column fans out slightly at its top to support the parapet, its railing missing. The round lantern room's metal — turned green from exposure to the elements — now surrounds an automated beacon. Worn patches mark the red cap of the tower.

A hundred yards away, at the tip of a small point of land is the old, red whistle house, the waves breaking just a few feet from its base.

"Lush greenery surrounding this long-abandoned station gives it a wild air."

51

Horse Island Lighthouse

"Most of the island has been cleared to create large fields, and the lighthouse and a few barns are the only buildings here."

Originally built in 1831 and later rebuilt in 1869, Horse Island Lighthouse dominates the lush, green landscape. Most of the interior of this private 30-acre island at the entrance to Sackets Harbor has been cleared to create large fields, and the lighthouse and a few barns are the only buildings here.

The keeper's house is a two-story tan brick structure with an addition built onto the back. A large deck extends from the addition, and there is much evidence of repairs to the house. The attached square tower rises nearly 50 feet and was made of tan bricks to match the house. Three of its walls, however, have been painted white, and small, square windows look out at various intervals. The square parapet is railed in white, and a bright red cap protects the lantern room.

TIBBETS POINT LIGHTHOUSE

Tibbets Point Lighthouse

"Though the whistle still works, it is no longer used because Wolfe Island residents complained the noise shook their homes."

The first light at Tibbets Point was built in 1827 to mark the meeting place of Lake Ontario with the St. Lawrence River. In 1854 the light was rebuilt, and its fresnel lens, though no longer used, is still in place today. The Tibbets Point Light is a round, white tower with only a few small windows interrupting its plastered sides. The tower fans out slightly to support the parapet. A sturdy iron railing circles the black, octagonal lantern room, and a small, white light mounted on the walkway has taken over the responsibilities of the tower's original lantern. The smooth plaster sides of the tower have cracked, leaving dark spidery lines etched into its surface. A small room attached to the back of the tower, a white, wooden keeper's house nearby, and a whistle house complete the lighthouse complex. And though the whistle still works, it is no longer used because Cape Vincent and Wolfe Island residents complained the noise shook their homes.

In 1988 the Tibbets Point Lighthouse Historical Society was formed to restore and preserve the light. The charming keeper's cottage has been turned into a youth hostel, giving hundreds of explorers a rare opportunity to sleep in the keeper's quarters. Plans for further development include a museum and other exhibits.

The lighthouse is situated on a bluff, and the view of the deep-blue lake and river, with its scattering of emerald islands, is beautiful. You can walk the grounds, enjoying spring lilacs or cool summer breezes blowing in off the lake.

Cape Vincent Breakwater Light

For more than 50 years beginning in 1900, the Cape Vincent Breakwater light stood on a wall of stone that jutted into the St. Lawrence River. In 1951 it was moved to its present site, adjacent to Market Street, where it greets visitors entering the town of Cape Vincent. Its white, wooden tower, which stands only 15 feet high, is topped with a square, black parapet and octagonal lantern room.

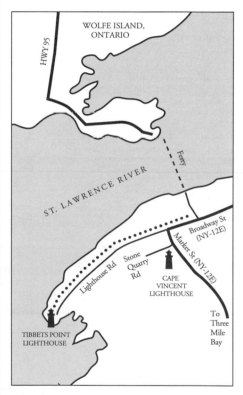

DIRECTIONS: From the intersection of the road to the Wolfe Island ferry and NY-12E (Broadway St.), drive southwest on 12E about 2½ blocks to the intersection of Market St. (12E) and Lighthouse Rd.

To get to the Cape Vincent Breakwater Light, turn left (south) onto Market (12-E) and go 0.6 miles to Stone Quarry Rd., on the right. The lighthouse is in front of the Cape Vincent City Building, on the right (west) side of Market St. near this intersection. You can turn onto Stone Quarry Rd. and park.

To visit Tibbets Point Lighthouse, from the Market St./Lighthouse Rd. intersection continue straight ahead (southwest) on Lighthouse Rd. (also called Tibbets Point Rd. and County Rd. 6) about 2.5 miles to its end, at the Tibbets Point Lighthouse.

East Charity Shoal Lighthouse

" A row of small portholes, looking like buttons, runs up one wall of the white tower, and rust has streaked the windward sides with orange. "

The tower of East Charity Shoal Light rests on a large, thick, square concrete foundation with a ladder built into one of the sides providing access for workers. Piles of dark stone border the eastern wall at lake level, and a wire railing surrounds the edge of the platform. Sitting squarely in the center of the structure is the octagonal tower. Its first level is cement, and its windows and doors have been boarded up. A short railing around the top edge of that level surrounds the metal tower, which tapers upward another 30 feet. A row of small portholes, looking like buttons, runs up one wall of the white tower, and rust has streaked the windward sides with orange. The black octagonal lantern room and its cap shelter an automated beacon that still warns navigators of the East Charity Shoal.

Rock Island Lighthouse

The first light on Rock Island — in the St. Lawrence River 4½ miles northeast of Clayton, New York — was constructed at the center of the tiny isle in 1848. In 1852 Bill Johnston, one the most famous keepers to work here, was appointed. Johnston was on the losing side during the 1838 Patriot War, an unsuccessful four-day attempt by a group of Canadians and Americans to take over Fort Wellington (near Prescott, Ontario) from the British. As a result Johnston was convicted but later pardoned, and he then rebuilt his life at the Rock Island Lighthouse.

In 1882 the light was increased in height and moved to the end of a 10-foot pier reaching into the river on the island's north shore, where it shone until its deactivation in 1958. The smooth, white walls of the round tower taper upward from the pier to a small ledge that encircles the structure halfway up. From there, the tower narrows slightly as it continues up to the black metal parapet and lantern room, supported with decorative arches beneath the walkway. A few small portholes set into the tower walls overlook the swiftly flowing river.

Smooth rock outcroppings line the riverbank behind the tower, and a few yards inland, a beautiful lawn dotted by shrubs and towering trees surrounds the keeper's house. That red two-story building was until recently privately owned.

Today the lighthouse complex — which also includes a smokehouse, carpenter's shop and boathouse — is owned by the New York State Office of Parks, Recreation and Historic Preservation. Facilities include a picnic area, but no restrooms, plus the lighthouse itself is not open. The only way to view it is from the water, and an excursion on tour boats that leave from Clayton, New York, is a good way to do exactly that. For group tours contact Thousand Islands State Park and Recreation Region, Keewaydin State Park, P.O. Box 207, Alexandria Bay, New York 13607; (315) 482-2593.

"Smooth rock outcroppings line the riverbank behind the tower, and a few yards inland, a beautiful lawn dotted by shrubs and towering trees surrounds the keeper's house."

Sunken Rock Lighthouse

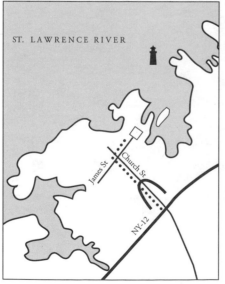

ST. LAWRENCE RIVER

James St.

Church St.

NY-12

The beautiful Thousand Islands area of the St. Lawrence Seaway is a mixture of large and small jewels set into the deep-blue river. One of the smallest islands, barely 20 by 20 feet, is home to Sunken Rock Lighthouse. As the name implies, there is an underwater rock, extremely dangerous to all ships passing in the area. But the lighthouse's foundation, surrounded by piles of stone, built up the submerged rock into a tiny island. At one end the small, white circular tower sits only inches from the water, its bright-green parapet and lantern room still warning ships of the danger lurking below. At the opposite end of the isle is a storage building.

You can get a good view of the light from shore or a close-up look from tour boats out of Alexandria Bay.

DIRECTIONS: From the intersection (marked by a traffic signal) of NY-12 and Church St. in Alexandria Bay, turn northwest onto Church and go 0.4 miles, under an arch, to James St. Turn right (east) onto James and go 1½ blocks to its end, near the tour boat docks. Street parking is available, and you can view Sunken Rock Lighthouse, out in the harbor, from the end of James Street or board a tour boat for a closer look.

Sisters Island Lighthouse

Sisters Island Lighthouse, in the St. Lawrence River, 12½ miles northeast from Alexandria Bay, is one of the area's most beautiful lighthouses. The two-story structure is made of cut-stone blocks of varying shades of gray. Rectangular 12-paned windows are trimmed in white, as are the eaves. Beneath the eaves, decorative supports and panels lend a delicate touch that is repeated in facades above the dormer windows.

From the inside of the house on the west wall, the three-story light tower rises just past the roofline. Square, white-trimmed windows are set into its gray walls, and as the tower rises, its corners taper inward to become deep grooves. A black metal railing on the parapet above also angles in at each corner, following the unusual pattern of the tower. The round, white lantern room is enclosed by windows and a round, black cap and ventilator ball.

A small yard provides a green buffer between the house and the rocky shore, which is protected by manmade walls in some areas. Look closely and you'll see that what is called Sisters Island is actually three tiny islands connected by walkways. The land here is barely able to support a few trees and bushes, leaving plenty of room for an occasional blue heron to glide in and visit.

In the river nearby is the rusty skeleton of the Third Brother Shoal Light, which predates the St. Lawrence Seaway. Today, a large bird, possibly an osprey, regally surveys its beautiful domain from a sprawling nest built atop the long-forgotten light.

"Beneath the eaves, decorative supports and panels lend a delicate touch that is repeated in facades above the dormer windows."

Crossover Island Lighthouse

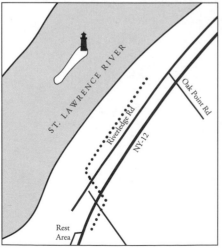

Crossover Island is a beautiful strip of land in the middle of the St. Lawrence River about halfway between Alexandria Bay and Morristown. Just wide enough for its red two-story house and small lawn, the island is dotted with tall trees and rimmed by a rocky shoreline. The tiny white tower of the Crossover Island Lighthouse dominates the island's eastern tip, and its red lantern room shows up brightly against the backdrop of turquoise waters.

Although this light is on private property, you can get excellent views from a road along the American shoreline.

DIRECTIONS: From NY-12 about 4.1 miles northeast of Chippewa Bay (0.3 miles past a rest area) and about 2.5 miles southwest of Oak Point Road, turn west (toward the river) onto an unmarked blacktop road and then almost immediately turn right (north) onto Riverledge Road, which parallels NY-12. Several viewing opportunities of the Crossover Island Lighthouse, to the left, come from Riverledge Road in the first ½ mile.

Ogdensburg Harbor Lighthouse

O gdensburg Harbor Light is on a small point of land, today called Lighthouse Point, that reaches into the St. Lawrence River. In 1749 the French established Fort La Presentation at the strategic locale, and Catholic missionaries used it as a base for their work. The French, however, weren't received with open arms by the area's Native Americans who, within a year, burned both the fort and two ships anchored in the harbor.

The first lighthouse here was built in 1834, and was replaced in 1900 by a second beacon, which still stands on the site of the old fort.

The keepers' residence is a small stone house with dormer windows poking out of its angled roof. A huge, 65-foot-high, square tower is attached to the front of the house. Halfway up, its rough stone walls change to smooth white, while also fanning out slightly to support the square parapet and 10-sided lantern room.

The lighthouse is now a private residence, but you can get a good view of it from the river or from the Canadian shore. Only a block from the lighthouse is the Frederick Remington Museum, which is filled with paintings of the surrounding area by one of America's premier artists and one-time resident of Ogdensburg.

" The French, however, weren't received with open arms by the area's Native Americans who, within a year, burned both the fort and two ships anchored in the harbor. "

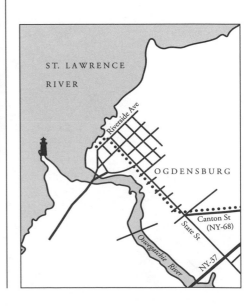

DIRECTIONS: From NY-37 in Ogdensburg, exit onto NY-68 (Canton St.) and go northwest 0.6 miles to the junction with State St. Turn right (north) onto State and drive about 0.7 miles to Riverside Ave. Turn left (west) onto Riverside and go one block to the city park. You can get a good view of the Ogdensburg Lighthouse across the bay. Another good view of this lighthouse comes from across the St. Lawrence River in Prescott, Ontario.

Windmill Point Lighthouse

"This beautiful tower originally was a working windmill, and its peaceful setting was the scene of the only military battle ever to take place in the county."

From its perch atop a bluff, the Windmill Point Lighthouse scans the beautiful ribbon of blue river passing by below. Swaying tops of trees growing from the riverbank are at eye level at the top of the bluff, and a lush expanse of lawn pulls back from the edge to surround the lighthouse. A split rail fence meanders across the grounds, and a stairway leads down the steep slope to the river's edge.

Curiously, this beautiful tower originally was a working windmill, and its peaceful setting was the scene of the only military battle ever to take place in the county. In 1838, during what was later called the Patriot War, a group of Canadian Rebels along with their American sympathizers crossed the river and set up camp near the towering windmill. The party hoped to wrest control of nearby Fort Wellington from the British, who learned of the plan and, along with local militia, surrounded the windmill area. After a bloody four-day battle, the rebels were defeated, but the "Battle of the Windmill" earned a permanent and prominent place in the area's history.

Thirty-five years after the battle, the beautiful gray stone tower was converted to a lighthouse. Today, a gravel path leads to a wide red door at the base of the tower. Each of the next four levels are marked by several square, red-shuttered windows set into the stone. The red parapet is supported by a crown of arches and braces that circle the tower. Windows at the front of the 10-sided lantern room stare across the bay to the town of Ogdensburg.

Fort Wellington, first built during the War of 1812, also still stands in nearby Prescott as a national historic site open to the public. In the summer, directed by period-costumed guides, you can explore the blockhouse, officers' quarters, and other displays and exhibits. On the third weekend in July, the Fort is the site of Canada's largest military spectacle, complete with mock battles and other re-enactments of past military life. And in December you can enjoy the "garrison Christmas" celebration.

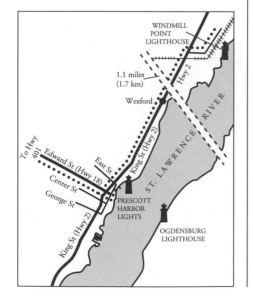

DIRECTIONS: From Highway 401 northeast of Brockville, exit (#716) onto Edward St. and go south 1.3 miles (2.1 km) to Highway 2 (King St.) in Prescott. Continue straight ahead on Edward across Hwy. 2 and go one block to Water St. Turn left (east) onto Water and go one block. Prescott Inner Harbor Light (p. 64) is next to the road on the right, at the city marina. Prescott Harbor Outer Light, a smaller light at the end of a rocky pier, is an entry light for the marina. Though only the outer light is an official Coast Guard beacon, both are worth seeing. Also, from shore here you can get good views of the Ogdensburg Harbor Lighthouse, across the St. Lawrence River, and the Windmill Point Light, downstream.

To get a closer look at the Windmill Point Light, go east from the marina on Water St. about ½ block to Highway 2 (King St.) Turn right (east) onto Hwy. 2 and go about 1.3 miles (2.1 km), through Wexford, to the first street after passing under a railroad overpass. Turn right (south) onto the unnamed street and go a short distance to where it jogs left. The lighthouse is just ahead on the right.

WINDMILL POINT LIGHTHOUSE

Prescott Harbor Lights

The 40-foot-high Prescott Inner Harbor Light is a replica of an old, generic lighthouse. The white, octagonal tower angles up to the wide, red lantern room, topped with a weathervane. Behind the angled panes of the lantern room, a fresnel lens donated by the Canadian Coast Guard continues to shine. (Another fresnel lens, from a saltwater light, is on display at the Coast Guard Station, nearby in Prescott.) A red railing that slips behind the base of the light leads to a beautiful view of Prescott Harbor. A set of double doors at the front open to a tourist information center inside.

Stretching out from shore is a narrow, rocky pier that is home to the Prescott Outer Harbor Light. That narrow, white tower rises about 20 feet to support a bright-green lantern and parapet.

DIRECTIONS and map, page 62.

PRESCOTT HARBOR OUTER LIGHT

PRESCOTT HARBOR INNER LIGHT

Wolfe Island Light

The East End Light on Wolfe Island is a small, square, white tower that tapers slightly upward 15 feet to a flat, red cap. The Middle Light, located on the south side of the island, is a 15-foot-tall, white steel cylinder topped by a red band. Both lights are topped with a small, automatic beacon.

Both lights are also on private property, and the best views of them come from the water.

WOLFE ISLAND EAST END LIGHT

Nine Mile Point Lighthouse

" The trip to this light is a miniadventure. Also, there is a unique combination floating museum/bed and breakfast nearby."

The Nine Mile Point Lighthouse on Simcoe Island is a round stone tower attached to one corner of a very large one-story building. Both structures have been painted pristine white, and an arched red door leads into the base of the tower. One tiny window peeps out from the center of each of the next three levels, and a round, red railing encircles the 12-sided lantern room nearly 50 feet above the water.

A concrete wall stretching along the shoreline near the light, rests on huge rock slabs close to the water. Leafy bushes have taken root near the wall, and their branches stretch out towards the water. Waves crash over both rock and concrete to naturally water the bushes and grasses nearby.

The trip to this light is itself a miniadventure. The town of Kingston provides free car ferry service to Wolfe Island, and from there you take a unique car ferry ride, via a cable strung to nearby Simcoe Island.

Also in Kingston is a unique combination floating museum/bed and breakfast — the 3,000-ton, retired Canadian Coast Guard icebreaker *Alexander Henry*. The ship is docked next to the Marine Museum of the Great Lakes, and both ship and museum are open April through December, daily from 10 a.m. to 5 p.m., and January through March, 10 a.m. to 4 p.m. Monday through Friday. The bed and breakfast operates from late spring through early fall. For further information or reservations, phone (613) 542-2261.

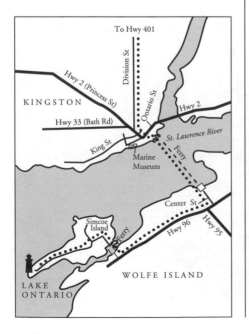

DIRECTIONS: From Highway 401 exit (#617) onto Division St. and go south 2.5 miles (4.0 km) to Highway 2 (Princess St.) in Kingston. Turn left (southeast) onto Hwy. 2 (Princess) and go about 0.7 miles (1.1 km) to Ontario St. Turn left (northeast) onto Ontario (Hwy. 2) and look for the Wolfe Island Ferry Dock, on the right. There is no charge for the Wolfe Island Ferry.

When you depart the ferry on Wolfe Island, go straight ahead (southeast) on Center St. to the junction with highways 95 and 96. Turn right (west) onto 95/96 go about 0.1 mile (0.16 km) to where 95 and 96 split. Follow Hwy. 96 straight ahead (west) about 3.4 miles (5.5 km) to a gravel road that turns right (north) to the cable ferry dock. A small fee is charged for autos and passengers.

When you depart the ferry, follow Simcoe Island's only road straight ahead (north) and then left (west) about 1.5 miles (2.4 km) to a tee in the road. Turn left (south) and follow the road as it winds back west about 2.2 miles (3.5 km) to the Nine Mile Point Lighthouse.

Note: From the junction of highways 95 and 96 on Wolfe Island, you can take Hwy. 95 south about 7 miles (11.3 km) to a boat dock and ferry to Cape Vincent, New York, where you can visit the Cape Vincent Light and the Tibbets Point Lighthouse.

NINE MILE POINT LIGHTHOUSE

Pigeon Island Light

" From the air this island usually looks as though it is caught in a snowstorm, with great drifts piled up along the shoreline. "

From the air this island usually looks as though it is caught in a snowstorm, with great drifts piled up along the shoreline. It is not snow but thousands of gulls that drop onto the island, covering all areas except two shallow pools of gray-green water at either end. The lightest birds blend into the rocky shoreline, but all stand out against the small patches of greenery that have been able to take a foothold here. The island's name indicates that at one time it was blanketed by passenger pigeons, not gulls.

Foundations are all that remain of the original buildings, but a steel tower still stands at the island's center. Its square, white skeleton frame supports a round, red tube leading up from the center of the structure to a small room with one narrow window. Topping the light is a round, red parapet and lantern room, their shiny red metal starkly contrasting with the natural wildness below.

Main Duck Island Lighthouse

The Main Duck Island Lighthouse sits on a small hook of land jutting from the northern shore of a 7-mile-wide, 15-mile-long island. Cement retaining walls protect part of the rocky shoreline from erosion, allowing a few trees and shrubs to gain a strong foothold. The lighthouse complex consists of two white-and-red, square buildings connected by a worn path to the lighthouse directly behind. The octagonal tower rests on a wide decorative foundation, with a few steps leading up to the small, red door at its base. As the tower rises, the edges of its angled sides gradually smooth out until they are barely discernible. At the summit an octagonal parapet surrounds the round lantern room, and both are painted bright red to match the entry door 60 feet below. A vertical row of four narrow windows peers out from both the north and south sides of the tower.

The surrounding Prince Edward County area has some of the best sand beaches on all of Lake Ontario. For mile after mile, golden dunes decorated with deep-green pines spill long trails of sand down into the light-turquoise lake. The dunes' beauty makes them popular weekend destinations, and most are easily approached from nearby roadways.

"For mile after mile, golden dunes decorated with deep-green pines spill long trails of sand down into the light turquoise lake."

False Duck Island Lighthouse

"The old tower was destroyed, pulled to the ground by a Canadian lighthouse tender, but that was not the end of the light."

The first light to shine at False Duck Island was built in 1829 and for more than 135 years illuminated its treacherous waters. A new, modern structure was built on the island in 1965, and a year later the old tower was destroyed, pulled to the ground by a Canadian lighthouse tender. That was not the end of the light, however. In 1967 its lantern and light were reinstalled atop a 30-foot-high limestone tower specially erected as a memorial to the seamen of Prince Edward County who had lost their lives in Lake Ontario waters.

The beautiful monument is now part of Mariner's Memorial Park and Museum, at South Bay on Quinte's Isle. A museum near the tower houses a collection of sailing artifacts and nautical displays, and scattered on the surrounding lawn are anchors, a wooden ship's mast, and two pilot houses from Great Lakes ships. The museum is open daily 10 a.m. to 5 p.m. July through Labor Day, and weekends only from Victoria Day through June 30 and Labor Day through Thanksgiving. The park surrounding the museum is open all year, and offers a picnic area and restrooms.

DIRECTIONS and map, page 72.

FALSE DUCK ISLAND LIGHTHOUSE MEMORIAL

Prince Edward Point Lighthouse

" The square, tapering tower abruptly ends at empty space, giving the structure a lonely, abandoned look. "

The original lighthouse on Prince Edward Point, built in 1881, is no longer in use. White paint has peeled in patches from the wood siding of both the two-story keeper's house and attached tower. The most distressing sign of neglect, however, is its missing lantern. Ten feet above the house's peaked roof, the square, tapering tower abruptly ends at empty space, giving the structure a lonely, abandoned look.

In front of the 112-year-old building stands a steel skeleton tower that has been in operation since 1959.

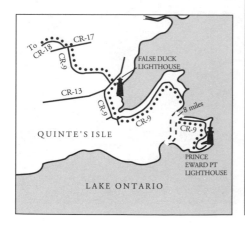

DIRECTIONS: From the junction of County Rd. 10 and County Rd. 18 in Cherry Valley, go left (south) on CR-10 about 5.1 miles (8.2 km) to the stop sign at CR-17 in Milford. Turn left (east) onto CR-17 and go one block to CR-9. Turn right (south) onto CR-9 and go about 2.8 miles (4.5 km) to the junction with CR-13. The Old False Duck Island Light and museum complex (p. 70) are to the left, across CR-13.

To get to Prince Edward Point Lighthouse, drive south from Mariners Park Museum on CR-9 (passing through a large limestone cut) about 7.3 miles (11.7 km) to a stop sign. Turn left onto the blacktop road, continuing to follow CR-9 about 5.9 miles (9.5 km) to the lighthouse. The road turns to good gravel at 0.6 mile, and the last 0.5 mile (0.80 km) is a narrow, but good two-track.

Point Petre Lighthouse

The first light on Quinte's Isle was built in 1833 at Point Petre, the southernmost tip of the island. In the late 1960s it was replaced by a new light and tragically blown up before any group could save it. The new Point Petre light is an unusual narrow concrete cylinder just wide enough to surround a door at its base. Alternating red and white stripes encircle the 50-foot-high tower, which widens at the top to form a small room in turn topped by a white beacon and red guardrail.

The light is in a restricted area, and you must have permission to visit (See Directions).

"The new Point Petre light is an unusual narrow concrete cylinder."

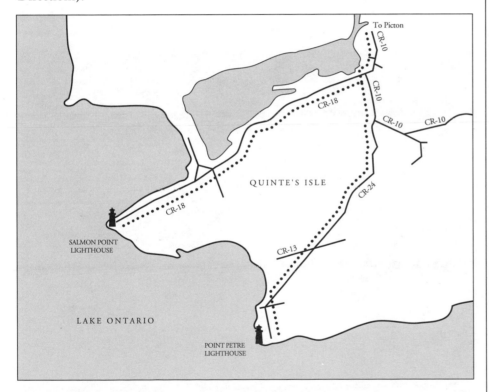

DIRECTIONS: From the intersection of Hwy. 33 and County Rd. 10 in Picton (on Quinte's Isle, south of Belleville), go south on CR-10 (also called East Lake Rd. or Cherry Valley Rd.) approximately 5.2 miles (8.3 km) to the stop light at the junction with CR-18 in Cherry Valley. To get to the Point Petre Lighthouse, turn left (south) and follow CR-10 another 1.2 miles (1.9 km) to the junction with CR-24. Turn right (southwest) onto CR-24 and go 6.4 miles (10.2 km) to its end at the Point Petre Light. This property is a Government Environmental Research Area, and you must ask permission to enter from the person in charge, at the house next to the light.

To get to the Salmon Point Lighthouse (p. 74), from the stop light at the intersection of CR-10 and CR-18 in Cherry Valley continue straight ahead (west), on CR-18, and drive about 4.4 miles (7.1 km) to an unnamed road marked with a sign pointing to Salmon Point. Follow that road about 2.4 miles (3.9 km) to the entrance to the Salmon Point Campground. There is a small per car charge ($1 in 1994) to visit the lighthouse. You can only view the outside; the interior is not open to the public.

Salmon Point Lighthouse

" The light sits on a concrete foundation touching the water's edge and open on one side to provide boat access beneath the house. "

The Salmon Point Lighthouse was built in 1871 to warn mariners of the dangerous shoals stretching out from the area, originally called Wicked Point because it was considered one of the most hazardous spots on Lake Ontario. The light sits on a concrete foundation touching the water's edge and open on one side to provide boat access beneath the house. The square, white wooden tower rises about 35 feet to support a square parapet and red, octagonal lantern room. Narrow windows look out from each side of the tower, and matching windows illuminate the small attached keepers' house.

The light was taken out of operation in 1917 and for a time was used as a residence and summer cottage. Today it stands unused within the boundaries of a private campground. For a small fee you can drive through and view the light.

DIRECTIONS and map, page 73.

Scotch Bonnet Lighthouse

cotch Bonnet Island is shaped like a comet, its rounded head leaving a trail of stone slabs to cut the waves. A border of light-green water marks the sudden shallows surrounding the island, which is only seven feet above Lake Ontario. Large, thin layers of gray stone create a shoreline so low at each end that even medium-size waves wash over it from edge to edge. A low protective wall surrounds a patch of green grasses and small shrubs, and in the center of this enclosure is the long-forgotten Scotch Bonnet Lighthouse.

It was built in 1856 and automated in 1912. In the 138 years of the light's watch, nature has done its utmost to destroy it. Only the tower and two walls of the keeper's house are standing — the rest of the structure lies scattered along the ground or hidden by the bushes. The tower has lost its lantern room, and its windward side — rough surface deeply scarred — has been so damaged by the elements that it is near collapsing.

In 1959 a steel skeleton was built near the tower. Since then, gulls and cormorants have taken over the island to such an extent that the Canadian government has declared the island off limits to humans during their nesting period.

"Scotch Bonnet Island is shaped like a comet, its rounded head leaving a trail of stone slabs to cut the waves."

Presqu'ile Point Lighthouse

"Several steps lead up to a uniquely shaped gothic arch entryway."

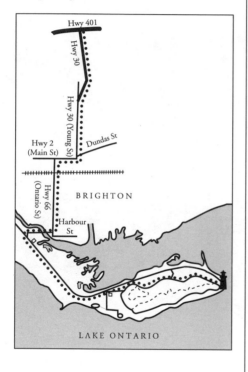

The Presqu'ile Point Lighthouse in Presqu'ile Provincial Park has guarded the waters off the point since 1840. The octagonal 67-foot-tall lighthouse sits atop a thick cement foundation, and several steps lead up to a uniquely shaped gothic arch entryway. The wood siding of the tower has been sheathed in metal from its base to about six feet up. A row of four small, square windows stretches up the white tower from above the doorway to where the walls curve outward to support the red-trimmed parapet. Unfortunately, nothing remains of the railing or lantern room. A small beacon atop the structure has continued to shine since the light was automated in 1952.

Inside the keeper's house, the park service runs a Museum of Natural History, with emphasis on wildlife and aquarium exhibits from the surrounding area. The museum is open from mid-May through June from 12 to 4 p.m. and daily in July and August from 9:30 a.m. to 5 p.m. Phone (613) 475-2204 for further information.

The shoreline in front of the lighthouse is gravelly, but four other Presqu'ile Provincial Park beaches that edge Lake Ontario nearby are ideal for swimmers.

DIRECTIONS: From Hwy. 401, exit (#509) onto Hwy. 30 and go south (the street name will change to George and then Young) 3 miles (4.8 km) to Main St. (Hwy. 2) in Brighton. Turn right (west) onto Main and go about 0.5 miles (0.8 km) to Ontario St. (Hwy. 66). Turn left (south) onto Ontario and drive 1.8 miles (2.8 km) to Harbour St. Turn right (west) onto Harbour and go 0.6 mile (1 km) to the entrance of Presqu'ile Provincial Park.

Enter the park (a fee is charged) and pick up a park map at an office on the left. From the park office go southeast (past roads to the beaches and the Marsh Boardwalk Trail) about 1.8 miles (2.8 km) to a "Y" junction. Take the right fork, go past the Camping Registration Office on the right, and continue about 0.3 mile (0.50 km) to the next fork in the road. You can take either fork, as the road circles back to this point. We took the left fork, and it was 2.3 miles (3.7 km) to the parking area at the lighthouse.

64

Brighton Range Lights

The old Brighton Range Lights have been replaced with modern cylinder lights.

PRESQU'ILE POINT LIGHTHOUSE

Cobourg East Pierhead Light

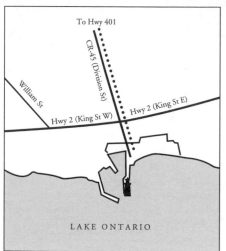

To Hwy 401

CR-45 (Division St)

William St

Hwy 2 (King St W)   Hwy 2 (King St E)

LAKE ONTARIO

The Cobourg East Pierhead Light rests at the end of a long cement pier. Its square, white base tapers abruptly upward to support a small red deck and beacon. Its mate, at the end of the sharply angled west pierhead, is a much smaller, white cylinder topped by a green platform and beacon.

Victoria Park, directly north of the east pier, is beautifully landscaped, with towering trees and lush lawns covering 20 acres. A new promenade and bicycle path edge Lake Ontario, and the park's white, sandy beach is a perfect place to cool off on a hot summer day. The park also includes a flower clock, playground, mini-golf course, picnic area, outdoor pool and camping area.

DIRECTIONS: From Highway 401 east of Toronto, exit (#474) onto County Rd. 45 (Division Street) and go south 3 miles (4.8 km) to its end, at Victoria Park on the shore of Lake Ontario in the town of Cobourg. You can walk from Victoria Park, which has both day-use and camping facilities, out onto the East Pier and to the light.

Toronto Harbour Light

The Toronto Harbour Light — also known as the Leslie Street Spit and officially listed as Toronto Harbour Aquatic Park Light (an aquatic park was planned but never developed) — marks the entrance to the bustling port city. The small, white cylinder marked with a red band at the top supports a small beacon at its summit. The light is perched on a manmade hill and fenced off inside Tommy Thomson Park, but you can get close-up looks from the walkway next to the fence.

You can either drive (see Directions) or take public bus service to the end of Leslie Street. From there, you take a shuttle van halfway out to the light, to where the spit is divided by a small canal with a pontoon-type swing bridge. The last mile is only accessible to pedestrians, and the walk to the light is across a wilderness haven in the midst of a major urban area. The roadway runs along a wooded area filled with wildflowers and shorebirds.

The view from the light is fantastic. Behind, the Toronto skyline shines in the sun, while several small islands, thick with trees, dot the deep-blue surrounding waters of the harbor.

Open only on summer weekends and holidays, this area is popular with city dwellers anxious to trade concrete and ashphalt for the lush greenery of the Leslie Street Spit.

> *"The walk to the light is across a wilderness haven in the midst of a major urban area."*

DIRECTIONS: From downtown Toronto follow the Gardiner Expressway east to its end at Lake Shore Blvd. Stay in the right lane and take the last exit from the Gardiner, which leads to a stop sign at Leslie St. Turn south onto Leslie and go about 0.4 miles to the parking area for Tommy Thomson Park. Leslie St. continues on into the park but is closed to vehicles. You can, however, catch a shuttle van, which runs about every 30 minutes from the parking area about halfway to the end of the spit. From there it is about a mile walk out to the land's end and the Harbour Light.

Note Tommy Thomson park is only open on weekends and holidays from June through August. For further information, call Metro Region Conservation at (416)-661-6600.

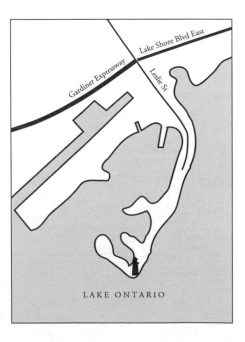

LAKE ONTARIO

Gibraltar Point Light

" According to local legend, several smaller land masses appeared during the 1850s as the waters quited in the wake of a passing hurricane. "

The Gibraltar Point Light, on Centre Island in Toronto's Inner Harbor, is a beautiful octagonal tower made of light-brown bricks. Tall bushes circle its base in soft green, and towering trees reach up beyond the light to frame the bright red parapet. The lantern still surveys the lush island, but it does not shine. In 1958 the Coast Guard replaced this light with a small skeleton tower nearby.

This serene and picturesque locale has a colorful history. Centre was the harbor's only island until, according to local legend, several smaller land masses appeared during the 1850s as the waters quieted in the wake of a passing hurricane. Shifting sands evidently had risen out of the lake, and Toronto residents, not wanting to lose the unusual gifts, built up the new islands to prevent their being lost in the next gale.

The light on Centre Island was Toronto's first, going into service in 1808. In 1815 its first lightkeeper, J. P. Rademuller, mysteriously disappeared, and two years later a skeleton believed to be his was discovered buried near the light. The island was later home to a baseball field from which Babe Ruth launched his first professional home run ... into the lake.

Today, you can take a ferry to the island and either rent a bike or take a shuttle train to the light. For further information call Metro Parks at (416) 392-8186. Another excellent vantage point, especially for photographers, is from aboard the *Jubilee Queen*. The harbor cruise boat makes a relaxing hour trip past both Toronto's beautiful skyline and the Gibraltar Point Light.

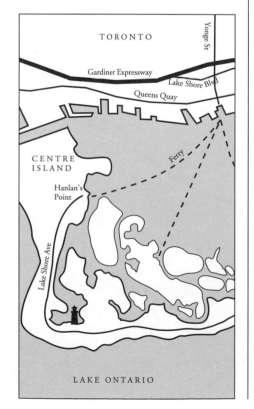

DIRECTIONS: Considering Toronto's size we have found it to be driver friendly. We recommend, however, that before you drive in Toronto, get a good city map and check your destinations in advance. You can expect heavy traffic during the morning and evening rush hours but not as heavy in the midmorning and afternoon periods.

Another alternative is to park outside of the city proper and use Toronto's excellent public transportation system to visit all three (Gibraltar Point, Queen's Wharf and Harbour) of the area lights.

If you drive into town and are coming from the west, enter Toronto on the Queen Elizabeth Way (Q.E.W.), which turns into the Gardiner Expressway through the downtown area. If you are coming from the east, enter on Highway 2, which turns into the Gardiner Expressway.

From the Gardiner in the downtown area about six blocks east of the CN Tower, exit onto Yonge St. and go south about 0.2 miles (0.3 km.) to Queens Quay, the street that runs along the waterfront area. Park in either direction along Queens Quay and walk to the Island Ferries Terminal, just west of Yonge St. on the waterfront.

Ferries depart for several different islands, so be sure to ask for the one to Hanlan's Point. Once at Hanlan's Point, catch a shuttle from the boat dock area to the Gilbraltar Point Lighthouse.

Note: Several harbor boat tours also depart from along the Queens Quay. Not all pass by the Gibraltar Point Lighthouse, however, so be sure to ask.

GIBRALTAR POINT LIGHT

Queen's Wharf Light

" The one lone surviving range light was saved and moved to its present place of honor, at the edge of a heavily traveled high-way in downtown Toronto. "

The first light on Toronto's Queen's Wharf was built in the 1830s, but by 1861 a new range light system on the wharf was guiding ships into the busy harbor. Those lights operated until 1912, when a new western harbor entrance made them unnecessary and nearly forgotten. They sat deteriorating until November 1929, when a lone surviving range light was saved and moved to its present place of honor, at the edge of a heavily traveled highway in downtown Toronto.

The brown wooden structure has tapered corners, an effect that makes it eight-sided. Windows are trimmed in white, and above the short second story, black shingles cover the roof. Rising from the center is the narrow parapet and lantern, surrounded by a small walkway. The lantern room, too, is enclosed by wood siding and is capped by a delicately curved roof, painted brown to match the lower stories. Although it's no longer apparent, the lantern was originally glazed in red glass to give its beam a color distinguishable from that of the other range light.

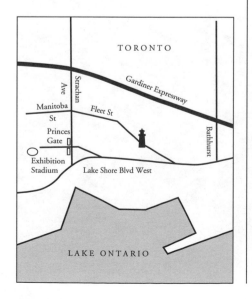

DIRECTIONS: Coming from the west, enter Toronto on the Queen Elizabeth Way (Q.E.W.), which turns into the Gardiner Expressway through the downtown area. Coming from the east, enter on Highway 2, which turns into the Gardiner Expressway.

From the Gardiner in the downtown area about six blocks east of the CN Tower, exit onto Yonge St. and go south about a block to Lake Shore Blvd. (If you are driving from the island ferry dock area, this intersection is two blocks north of Queens Quay on Yonge.) Turn right (west) onto Lake Shore and go approximately 1.7 miles (2.7 km) to the Princes Gate, the large stone arch entrance to Exibition Stadium. Just before reaching the Princes Gate, turn right (north) onto Strachan Ave. and go one block to Fleet St. (At this intersection a street sign reads "Manitoba," which is the name of the street leading west.) Turn right (east) onto Fleet and drive about 0.1 mile (.16 km) to the lighthouse, in a park on the right.

QUEEN'S WHARF LIGHT AS IT APPEARED IN 1926. (Photo courtesy of the Metropolitan Toronto Reference Library)

Oakville Lights

"Townsfolk, including school children, watched as the light suffered the ultimate indignity. Unable to retain its precarious perch, it fell into the raging waters."

The first lighthouse in Oakville was built in 1837 in response to increased lake traffic in the area. For nearly 50 years it served the community well, guiding lake ferries into the port of Oakville. But in April 1886, a violent spring storm — with howling winds and 30-foot waves — slammed into the area. By the second day of the storm, the pier had been breached and the lighthouse at its end was in danger. Townsfolk, including school children, watched as the light suffered the ultimate indignity. Unable to retain its precarious perch, it fell into the raging waters. In the months that followed, the pier was rebuilt, but the lighthouse wasn't replaced until 1889.

In early 1960s the light was taken out of service and moved ashore to its current location at a private marina. Standing about 25 feet high, the wooden six-sided structure narrows slightly toward its red lantern room, which is surrounded by a red-railed steel walkway.

Oakville Harbor now has two matching lights, on the piers at either side of the mouth of 16 Mile Creek. The round, white cylinders topped in red guide sailors into the harbor, upholding the tradition started more than 150 years ago.

■ DIRECTIONS: From the Queen Elizabeth Way (QEW) southwest of Toronto, exit (#118) onto Trafalgar St. and go south approximately 1.4 miles (2.2 km) to Lakeshore Rd. (Hwy. 2) in Oakville. Turn right (west) onto Lakeshore and drive about 1.1 miles (1.7 km) to Forsythe St., the first street after crossing Sixteen Mile Creek. Turn left (south) onto Forsythe, then almost immediately turn left (east) onto an unnamed road that goes down the hill into Shipyard Park. The old lighthouse is in a private, fenced-in area on the riverbank adjacent to the parking area.

QEW
QEW
Trafalgar
Chisholm St
Forsythe St
Lakeshore Rd (Hwy 2)
Lakeshore Rd (Hwy 2)
16 Mile Creek

LAKE ONTARIO

Burlington Canal Range Light and Main Lighthouse

In 1832 a newly opened canal split the Burlington beach and made the town more accessible to lake traffic. Six years later a wooden lighthouse on the canal's south side was lit and began guiding ships into the waterway.

As steam power became increasingly common on the lake, ships sometimes endangered the very lighthouses that protected them. Sparks from their smokestacks often showered down on wood towers and piers, occasionally with dire consequences. In 1856, for instance, sparks from a passing steamer spread

> *"Ships sometimes endangered the very lighthouses that protected them."*

BURLINGTON MAIN LIGHTHOUSE

"Narrow slit windows cut into each level give it a fortress-like appearance."

over the Burlington pier, and strong winds fanned them into a blaze that consumed a ferry house, two lightkeeper's buildings, and the wooden lighthouse.

The town erected a new, more-fire-resistant stone lighthouse that still stands at the canal's edge, behind a lift bridge that stretches over the waterway. The four-story-high, round structure is made of long, light-brown stone blocks, and the narrow slit windows cut into each level give it a fortress-like appearance. A round iron-railed parapet surrounds the 12-sided lantern room with windows at the front and metal panels in the rear. Lines of rust from the metal roof have run over the edge of the parapet to stain the stone below. Sitting about 75 feet away is a red, brick keeper's house.

About 300 yards away is the Burlington Canal Range Light, which stands at the end of a pier that juts from the canal mouth into Lake Ontario. The 32-foot-high metal structure with a square base narrows to support a small, square walkway and red beacon. A tall red-and-white steel skeleton radio tower extends far above the light. On the opposite pier, a small, round steel tower, painted white with a red stripe at the top, also helps mark the harbor entrance.

BURLINGTON CANAL RANGE LIGHT

DIRECTIONS: From the Queen Elizabeth Way (QEW) on the eastern edge of Hamilton, exit (#88) onto Centennial Parkway and go north, toward Lake Ontario. About two blocks after the exit, Centennial jogs sharply left (west) and becomes Confederation Drive. Go about 0.5 miles (0.8 km.) on Confederation to a T-intersection. Turn right (north), continuing to follow Confederation about two blocks to Van Wagners Beach Rd. Turn left (west) onto Van Wagners and follow it one mile (1.6 km) to Beach Blvd. Turn right (north) onto Beach and go 2.3 miles (3.7 km) to Eastport Dr. Turn right (west) onto Eastport and go 0.2 miles (0.3 km) to a narrow blacktop road just before the lift bridge. Turn left (south) onto the blacktop road and follow it to the right and down a hill to the parking area next to the pier. The main Burlington Light is to the right, next to the lift bridge. The Burlington Canal Range Light is at the end of the pier, also to the right. You can walk from the parking area under the lift bridge and out to the range light.

Port Dalhousie Range Lights

At the turn of the century, Port Dalhousie was a hectic, bustling town, with thousands of day-trippers from Toronto filling passenger ferries and making the 25-mile crossing to the area's parks and beaches. Today, a ferry no longer connects Port Dalhousie to the shore holding the modern towers of Toronto visible across the water. The parks are still there, though, and at one — Lakeside Park — you can ride on an original 19th-century carousel at a nostalgic 19th-century price — a nickel.

The Port Dalhousie Range Lights, too, stand as a scenic reminder of a bygone era. The first Rear Range Light was built in 1852 and was replaced in 1893 by a new light. That light stood for only five years before being destroyed by lightning during a storm. A few months later, the captain of the schooner *Leighton,* unaware the light had burned down, ran aground in the bay.

In the fall of 1898, a new light was finally erected, and it still stands today. Gradually tapered walls stretch up 40 feet from its wide octagonal base. White vertical siding provides an interesting pattern, and each of the small windows and the door have cozy peaks protruding above them. A green lantern room and parapet top the structure. The shore surrounding the light has been dotted with newly planted trees.

At the end of a 1500-foot pier that pokes into Lake Ontario's sparkling blue waters is the Front Range Light. The square light has a wide, green base, white, tapered tower, and green lantern room. Next to the narrow pier, Port Dalhousie's popular Michigan Beach stretches along the shore.

Both lighthouses were automated in 1968, and 20 years later, the light from

> *"The Port Dalhousie Range Lights stand as a scenic reminder of a bygone era."*

"Next to the narrow pier, Port Dalhousie's popular Michigan Beach stretches along the shore."

the rear range was extinguished after 136 years of service.

An excellent way to view these lights plus the light at Port Weller is aboard the tour boat *Garden City*. The cruise begins with a tour of Port Dalhousie's quaint harbor, then continues along Lake Ontario's shore to the entrance to the fourth Welland Canal in Port Weller. The *Garden City* passes the light and Coast Guard Station there, which is the best way to view them, as they are off-limits by land. The tour continues up into the first lock, where you get a fascinating, close-up look at the workings of the canal.

PORT DALHOUSIE OUTER RANGE LIGHT

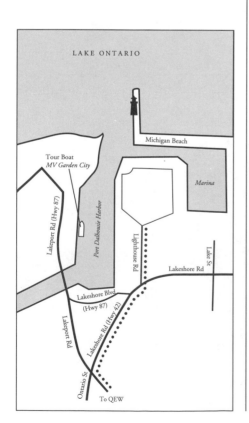

DIRECTIONS: From the Q.E.W. in St. Catherines, exit (#46) onto Highway 44 (Lake St. then Lakeport Rd.) and go north approximately 1.3 miles (2.1 km) to Lakeshore Rd. (Hwy. 42). Turn right (northeast) onto Lakeshore Rd. and go a little more than a block to Lighthouse Rd. (just past the junction with Lakeshore Blvd., on the left). Turn left (north) onto Lighthouse Rd. and go about 0.3 miles (0.4 km) to its end in the parking area next to the Port Dalhousie Harbor. The Port Dalhousie Range Lights are directly north of the lot.

The best way to view the Port Dalhousie Range Lights and the Port Weller Outer Light is from the tour boat *M.V. Garden City*, which departs from the west side of the harbor. To get there, backtrack along Lighthouse Rd. and briefly on Lakeshore Rd. to the junction with Lakeshore Blvd. (Hwy. 87). Turn right (west) onto Hwy 87 and follow it (on Lakeshore Blvd., then right [north] onto Lakeport Rd.) approximately 0.5 miles (0.8 km). The *M.V. Garden City* tour boat parking is on the right, just past the Royal Canadian Legion building.

For information or reservations contact Fortune Navigation, P.O. Box 2452, St. Catherines, Ontario L2M 7M8; (416) 646-2234.

PORT DALHOUSIE INNER RANGE LIGHT

Port Weller Light

> *"Its parapet-style roof caught rainwater, filtered it, and drained it into a cistern beneath the house."*

The Port Weller Light watches over a manmade harbor and guards the entrance to one of the most famous engineering feats on the Great Lakes. Stretching inland from the light is the Welland Canal, which cuts through the Niagara escarpment and bypasses the formidable falls, thereby opening up Lake Erie and the upper Great Lakes to outside shipping traffic. The canal was first dug from Port Dalhousie to Lake Erie in 1829. Over the next 103 years, improvements and new entrances expanded the waterway so that it now stretches from Port Weller — the fourth and newest entrance, on Lake Ontario — to Port Colborne, on Lake Erie.

The Port Weller Light is a white steel structure at the end of a narrow concrete pier. Near shore the pier is wide enough to accommodate the keeper's house, its surrounding large yard, and a thick row of trees behind. The house, built in 1931, is an Art Deco style, white one-story concrete building that had a unique water supply system. Its parapet-style roof caught rainwater, filtered it, and drained it into a cistern beneath the house. However, during the 1940s soot from passing ships contaminated the collected rainwater, and so water had to be pumped directly from the canal.

The first lighthouse keeper here, Cyril Williamson, and his wife, Ethel, earned an international reputation as ham radio operators. Their broadcasts plus magazine articles about them brought visitors from around the world to their home on the canal. And one Christmas they even described their life at the lighthouse in a live broadcast over BBC radio in England. Today, the Coast Guard uses the building as a search and rescue office.

Cutting inland from the light, the pale-green waters of the Welland Canal reflect the darker greens of trees that follow the length of the breakwall on both sides of the waterway.

Since this light cannot be closely approached from land, the best way to view it is during a spectacular boat tour that leaves from Port Dalhousie (see p. 87) and moves down the Welland Canal and through the #1 lock.

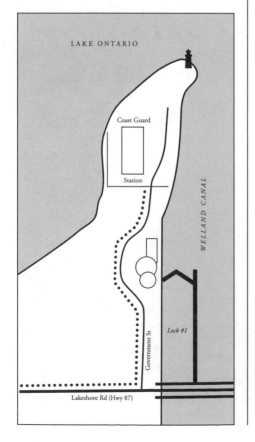

DIRECTIONS: From the junction of Hwy. 87 (Lakeshore Rd). and Lighthouse Rd. in Port Dalhousie (see map, p. 88), go east on Hwy. 87 2.3 miles (3.7 km) to the Welland Canal. Just before crossing the canal, turn left (north) onto Government St. and drive about 0.9 miles (1.4 km.) to its end, at the gate of the Port Weller Coast Guard Station. Although you cannot enter the active station, you can see the Outer Light from the gate. To get a close-up view, take the *M.V. Garden City* tour boat (see Directions, p. 88).

PORT WELLER LIGHT

Niagara River Range Lights

The Niagara River Range Lights, which mark the mouth of the beautiful Niagara River, both sit on the shore at the historic town of Niagara-on-the-Lake. The front range light is a square white 30-foot-high tower that angles sharply upward to support a wide red parapet and lantern room. The rear range light — also a square white tower topped with a red lantern room and parapet — matches its companion, except that it's about 15 feet taller.

Because of the area's strategic locale, in 1720 the French chose the eastern (now American) bank as the site to build Fort Niagara, which for nearly 40 years was their most important military establishment on the Niagara Frontier. In 1759, during the French and Indian War, the fort was surrendered to the British, who held it for two decades.

The British in turn, gave up the fort to the Americans after the Revolutionary War, then from 1797-1799 constructed another fort on the opposite (now Canadian) shore and named it Fort George. Today Fort George is a National Historic Site, and you can explore its restored buildings and fortifications on the bluff overlooking the river. Fort George is open daily from mid-May through June 30, 9 a.m. to 5 p.m.; July 1 through Labor Day, 10 a.m. to 6 p.m.; and Labor Day to Oct 31, 10 a.m. to 5 p.m. During the rest of the year, it is open by appointment only.

A few miles down the Niagara Parkway in Queenston Heights Park is Brock's Monument National Historic Site. An ornate 100-foot-high tower was built on the site of a decisive battle in the War of 1812 in which the governor general of Canada, Sir Isaac Brock, a brilliant military strategist and ally and friend of the Shawnee leader Tecumseh, was killed. You can walk the battlefield and also climb the monument for a panoramic view of the surrounding area. The park is open daily from mid-May to Labor Day, 10 a.m. to 6 p.m. There is no admission charge.

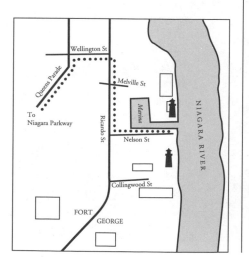

DIRECTIONS: Take the Niagara Parkway north from Niagara Falls to the town of Niagara-On-The-Lake. As you enter Niagara-On-The-Lake, the Niagara Parkway changes to Queens Parade and passes Fort George, on the right. Queens Parade then curves left and in about ½ block intersects Wellington Street. Turn right (east) onto Wellington and go two blocks to Ricardo St. Turn right (south) onto Ricardo and drive two blocks to Nelson St. Turn left (east) onto Nelson and go to its end, at the Niagara River. The front range light is to the left and the rear range light is one block away, to the right.

NIAGARA RIVER REAR RANGE LIGHT

Point Abino Lighthouse

"The lightkeepers here had to put on hip waders and slog through the shallow water to get to their post."

In the late 1800s, fixed buoys marked the dangerous shelf of rock that stretches out from Point Abino. In 1907 they were replaced by a lightship, which tragically sank with all hands aboard during a fierce November 1913 storm. Five years later the location of the hazardous reef was finally marked from shore, with the construction of the Point Abino Lighthouse.

The beautiful, still-operational light stands off the tip of the small peninsula 10 miles across the lake from Buffalo, New York. The structure rests on a wide cement platform about four feet above Lake Erie. The tip of the peninsula's rugged shoreline gradually spills large rocks down to, then into the water. At the point where water and stone meet is the first step of the stairway leading up to the lighthouse. The lighthouse, then, is essentially offshore and, except for that lone step, surrounded by water. And, since the mainland behind the light is private property, the lightkeepers here had to put on hip waders and slog through the shallow water to get to their post.

The one-story brick dwelling is painted a crisp white accented by small touches of red — on the keystone of the arches above all windows and on the small shades extending out from a few of the rear windows. A wide band of gray trim that surrounds the base of the house matches the trim around its flat roof. The six-story tower commands the southern half of the structure. Where the square tower begins to rise, a small, round window sheltered by an overhang peers out from each side. From there the tower narrows slightly as it completes its rise. Each level is marked by narrow windows — a brush of red on the trim above each one — that reflect the design of the house below. The top of the tower arches out to support the square parapet, which is surrounded by an intricate railing. You can see the fresnel lens through the panes of the 10-sided lantern room, and a red metal roof tops the beautiful structure.

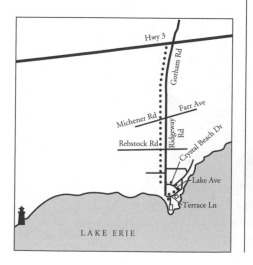

DIRECTIONS: The land around this light is private, but you can get good views from a public park across the bay. To get to it, turn south from Hwy. 3 approximately 7.5 miles (12.1 km) west of Fort Erie onto Niagara County Road 116 (Gorham Rd.) and go about 2.2 miles (3.5 km) to Rebstock Rd. Continue straight ahead on County Rd. 116 (now also Ridgeway Rd.) about 0.6 mile (1 km) to Crystal Beach Dr., on the left. Turn left (east) onto Crystal Beach Dr. and go one block to Lake Ave. Turn right (south) onto Lake and go one block to Terrace Lane. Turn right (west) onto Terrace, go about ½ block, and turn left (south) into Crystal Beach Park. The Point Abino Lighthouse is on the point, west across the bay from the west side of the parking area.

POINT ABINO LIGHTHOUSE

Port Colborne Inner and Outer Lights

In 1834 the first lighthouse in Port Colborne was built at the end of a long pier at the entrance to the Welland Canal. As the entrance to the canal changed, so did its lights, and a second pier and lighthouse later replaced the first light. That light in turn was replaced in 1903 by the lighthouse that still stands on the north breakwall. The south breakwall outer light was built in 1928, at which time an old range light farther inland was torn down.

With the construction of the south breakwall light, the north breakwall light became the Inner Light of Port Colborne. A long white building adjoins its square cement first level, and its white tower stretches up another two stories. A red parapet and lantern room protect the light, which still guides ships into the canal.

The Outer Breakwall Light, also still operating, is a short, square, white building trimmed in red and topped with a small room that supports the red parapet and lantern.

An added attraction in the area is the Historical and Marine Museum in downtown Port Colborne. The museum's main building, a beautiful Georgian-style home built in 1869, is filled with nautical and local-history treasures. The museum complex also includes a log school and home from the early 1800s, a working blacksmith shop, and the wheelhouse from the tug *Yvon Dupre Jr.* In a 1920s-era room in another historical home on the site, you can take afternoon tea, complete with jam and biscuits. There is no admission charge to the museum complex, which is open daily, noon to 5 p.m., May through December.

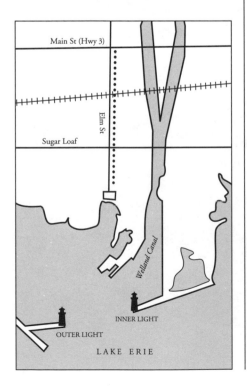

DIRECTIONS: From Hwy. 3 (Main St.) in Port Colborne, turn south onto Elm St. (three blocks west of the Welland Canal) and follow it 1.3 miles (2.1 km) to its end at Lakeview Park. Although the lights are quite a distance off shore, you can still photograph them from here. We chose to get a closer look at these two lights plus the Point Abino Lighthouse by using a charter boat. The rates are very reasonable and we highly recommend our charter boat captain, listed on page 124.

PORT COLBORNE INNER LIGHT

PORT COLBORNE OUTER LIGHT

Mohawk Island Lighthouse

" The island area held anoth-er danger that it tragically revealed in December 1932. "

The Mohawk Island Lighthouse was once an important beacon, guiding ships destined for the harbor of Port Maitland and the first Welland Canal. Built in 1848 on the flat strip of rocky land that forms the only island in eastern Lake Erie, the light helped ships avoid a dangerous reef nearby and find safe harbor in a storm.

The island area held another danger that it tragically revealed in December 1932. Keeper Richard Foster and his 26-year-old son James had just closed up the light for the season when they received word that their family home on the mainland was on fire. They hurriedly set out to make the 1½-mile crossing in their motorboat, but became trapped in an ice flow and were driven off course. Their frozen bodies and their boat were later found on the shores of Point Abino, 27 miles away.

The following year, shaken authorities decided to keep the light unmanned and converted it to battery power. By that time the light had become less important since the Welland Canal entrance had been moved to Port Colborne, 12 miles from the island. Finally, in 1969 the responsibilities of its beacon were replaced by a floating buoy.

Today, largely because of vandalism, all that remains of the Mohawk Island Light are the weathered stone walls of its dwelling and the shell of the seven-story tower, its lantern room and walkway gone.

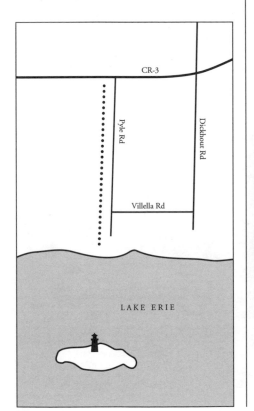

DIRECTIONS: You can view the Mohawk Island Lighthouse from shore between Dunnville and Port Colborne. From the intersection of Highway 3 and County Rd. 3 (about 5 miles [8 km] west of Port Colborne where Hwy. 3 turns north to Wainfleet) go west on County Road 3, which runs close to the Lake Erie shore, to HN-65 in Lowbanks. From the intersection of Co. Rd.-3 and HN-65, continue west on Co. Rd. 3 approximately 4 miles (6.4 km) to Pyle Rd. Turn left (south) onto Pyle and go 0.6 miles (0.96 km) to its end at Villella Road. You can get a very good view of the lighthouse from the end of the road right-of-way.

Port Maitland Range Light

The Port Maitland Range Light sits at the end of a long concrete pier that juts into Lake Erie at the mouth of the Grand River. Built on a thick, square platform five feet above the pier, the tower has a white square base with a large door providing access to the interior. Its second and third levels gradually taper to support the lantern room, which is surrounded by a square black parapet. The octagonal lantern room still shines its green electric beacon out into Lake Erie. A series of metal poles support electric wires running out to the light, which makes it seem less isolated than most pier lights.

Adjacent to the pier is Esplanade Park, with a playground and picnic area.

" It seems less isolated than most pier lights. "

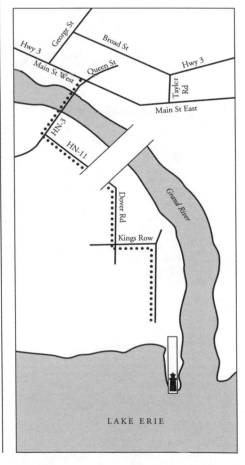

LAKE ERIE

DIRECTIONS: From Hwy. 3 in Dunnville, make your way to the interesection of Main St. and HN-3 (Queen St.) as follows: If you are coming from the west, where Hwy. 3 turns left onto George St. continue straight (east), on Main, and go about 0.6 miles (0.96 km) to HN-3. If you are coming from the east, turn left (south) onto Taylor Rd. and go about 1½ blocks to Main. Turn right (west) onto Main and go approximately one mile (1.6 km) to HN-3.

From the intersection of Main and HN-3, turn south onto HN-3 and go (over the bridge on the Grand River) about 0.7 miles (1.1 km) to HN-11 (Dover Rd.). Turn left (southeast) onto HN-11 and drive approximately 3.6 miles (5.7 km) to Kings Row. Turn left (east) onto Kings Row and follow it, as it turns right and parallels the river, about 0.7 mile (1.1 km) to a parking area, on the left. The Pier Head light is just to the right of the parking area.

Port Dover Front Range Light

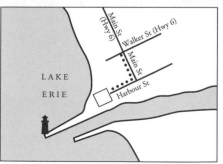

The Front Range Light at Port Dover is at the end of a long pier stretching into Lake Erie at the mouth of the Lynn River. Its steel-sided, square base tapers upward to support a small lantern room with a steel walkway surrounding it. A small ventilation pipe perches atop the lantern room, and a door at ground level provides access to the tower.

DIRECTIONS: From the intersection (marked by a traffic signal) of Main and Walker streets (both are part of the route, Hwy. 6) in Port Dover, go east on Main one block to Harbour St. Turn right (south) onto Harbour and drive one block to the parking area. The Port Dover Range Light is straight ahead, at the end of the pier.

Long Point Lighthouse

Long Point is a dangerous strip of land hooking its way into Lake Erie that has lured dozens of ships to their doom in the past three centuries. Legends of buried treasure, pirates and a headless ghost still rise out of the boggy marshes and ever-shifting sands of the beautiful point. Many a ship's hull and cargo — including perhaps a treasure chest or two — are buried here say the stories. One tells of a British captain who was afraid his ship's payroll might fall into the hands of the Americans during the War of 1812. He anchored in the calm waters of the bay and, with a few trusted crew members, came ashore to bury the chestful of gold. Later, the ship was lost in battle, but two crewmen survived to tell the tale of buried treasure.

In 1830 the first lighthouse was built on Long Point, but the fierce weather that threatened ships in the area also wreaked havoc on the light tower, and it was replaced in 1843 by a second light. That light served for 73 years before it too succumbed to the pounding waves. The light that continues to guard the coast of this rugged area was built in 1916, and the tower stands firm thanks to structural changes around its base. Its white stone ends at a lantern that today is

" Legends of buried treasure, pirates and a headless ghost still rise out of the boggy marshes and ever-shifting sands of the beautiful point. "

"A 19-year-old, for no particular reason, made a 12-hour walk across the frozen lake."

fully automated. A long catwalk runs over the shallow ponds that surround the tower. The keeper's house stood until 1983, when it too was finally undermined by waves.

Countless bodies from shipwrecks have washed up on the sands here, and it was sometimes the lighthouse keeper's responsibility to find and bury victims of the lake. Perhaps the most tragic wreck occurred on November 25, 1860, when the *Jersey City* broke up during a bitter gale and its 22 crew members were forced to swim for their lives. Twenty made it to shore but were confused as to where they were in relation to the safety and warmth of the lighthouse. One group went one way down the beach, another group headed in the opposite direction, and a third group stayed put. Those who didn't move quickly froze to death, but their shipmates didn't fare much better. Only five, barely alive, made it to the lighthouse. The lighthouse keeper found the others dead — frozen in various positions, some clutched in a final embrace.

Nature has not been the only source of danger here. Not long after the light was first erected, pirates would set up a fake light halfway down the point, tricking captains into turning their ships early. The ships nearly always ran aground and broke up, leaving the pirates to plunder cargo and even steal from bodies that washed ashore.

One sailor suffered a particularly grisly fate. In the 1880s the crew of a steamer spotted another ship sinking off the point. In the haste to lower a life boat, a crewman's head was severed. His body was buried on the point, giving rise to a legend that the area is haunted by a headless ghost.

The life of a lighthouse keeper here, however, was for the most part routine and did even have its share of pleasant surprises. During the winter of 1912, for instance, the keeper received an unexpected visitor — Walter Lick, a 19-year-old from Erie, Pennsylvania, who had for no particular reason made a 12-hour walk across the frozen lake. Three men have since repeated the feat.

Today, Long Point and its light are off limits to visitors. One large strip of land has been set aside as a National Wildlife Area, and other large tracts are under private ownership, making an approach to the light impossible. You can, however, get good views from off shore.

We had the good fortune to be able to fly over the point, which afforded us an absolutely spectacular view. Golden strips of sand were fringed with grasses, and the entire point was laced with narrow strips of turquoise water cutting across the greens and golds of the land.

Old Long Point Lighthouse

The Old Long Point Lighthouse, built in 1879, was originally called the Cut Light, as it marked a natural channel that had been cut through the Long Point peninsula during a storm. For a time, ships had the option of sailing through that channel to avoid the extreme dangers of the shallows that surround the point. But the channel was unreliable, constantly filling in with shifting sands during the frequent storms here. Finally, during a 1906 blow, the cut filled in completely and could no longer be used. The Cut Light, however, continued to shine for 10 more years. Today it is a private residence.

The house and tower have been painted a unique bright-green and are accented by the olive-green ashphalt shingles of the house's roof.

The square, gradually tapering tower covers half the roof, and narrow four-pane windows mark each of its two levels. The tower has been sided with wood shingles painted light-green. In some areas, the siding has been replaced with olive-green shingles that match the house's roof and give the tower a mottled appearance.

Large patches of bright-green paint have weathered off the lantern room to expose its wood shingles. The square lantern room is slightly wider than the tower, and several wooden supports help make up decorative trim around its bottom edge. Windows wrapped around the perimeter of the lantern room are now boarded up, and a dark-brown ashphalt-shingled roof also helps protects it.

"The Old Long Point Lighthouse originally marked a natural channel that had been cut through the Long Point peninsula during a storm."

DIRECTIONS: From Hwy. 3 about midway between St. Thomas and Simcoe, turn south onto Hwy. 59 and go about 30 miles (48 km) to the intersection with Hwy. 42. Continue straight (south) on Hwy. 59 another 5.1 miles (8.2 km) to the Long Point Provincial Park entrance. The Old Long Point Lighthouse is on the left just before entering the park, and though it is on private property you can get a good view from the road in that area.

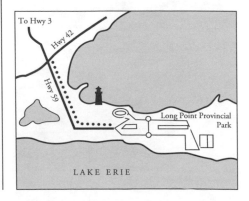

Port Burwell Main Lighthouse

" In 1852 Alexander Sutherland became keeper here, beginning a tradition of family service that was to continue an astonishing one hundred years."

The pride of Port Burwell, Ontario, is a 65-foot-tall light tower at the mouth of Otter Creek. Built in 1840 on a gentle rise near the lakeshore, it is Canada's oldest wooden lighthouse and the first Ontario light to shine over Lake Erie. In 1852 Alexander Sutherland became keeper here, beginning a tradition of family service that was to continue an astonishing one hundred years. Three of Alexander's sons and two grandsons followed in his footsteps, one succeeding the other until 1952, when the light was put out of service. Along with the main light, the Sutherlands had to service pierhead lights as well.

As did all keepers on the lakes, the Sutherlands wrestled often with Mother Nature. But Alexander's third son, John, seemed to lose more than his share of matches. On several occasions as he attempted to reach the pierhead, crashing waves washed him into the water, forcing him to swim back to the pier. Several times he suffered severe injuries, and once dragged himself down the length of the pier with a broken leg. His courage, unshakeable confidence, devotion to duty, and evidently powerful swimming ability didn't go unnoticed, however. In 1935 he was awarded the King George Jubilee Medal, followed several years later by the George VI Imperial Service Medal.

In 1965, 13 years after its beacon had stopped shining, the town of Port Burwell received title to the lighthouse. But a century and a quarter of Lake Erie weather had taken its toll, and by 1986 a major renovation became necessary. Mennonite craftsmen working with 19th-century hand tools refurbished the structure in areas weakened through the years. Also, the tower's original spiral stairway was changed to a zig-zag pattern for the safety of visitors.

You can climb the tower up to the now-ceremonial electric light that shines from the lantern. Across the street is a museum that houses a fine collection of lighthouse lenses and maritime artifacts.

PORT BURWELL MUSEUM

DIRECTIONS and map, page 106.

PORT BURWELL MAIN LIGHTHOUSE

Port Burwell Approach Light

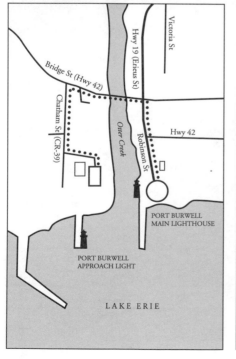

The Port Burwell Approach Light stands at the end of a long, improved pier with railings and benches stretching its length. The 15-foot-tall, pyramidal concrete tower ends at a flat roof supporting a narrow skeleton tower that rises up another 10 feet to a red beacon.

DIRECTIONS: From Hwy. 3 between St. Thomas and Simcoe, take Hwy. 19 south to its end at Hwy. 42 (Bridge St.) in Port Burwell. (As you enter Port Burwell, Hwy. 19 is named Erieus St., which bears right [west]. The intersection with Hwy. 42 is marked by a bridge, on the right.) Continue straight ahead (south), now on Robinson St., another 0.2 miles (0.32 km) to the Port Burwell Main Lighthouse (p. 104), on the right.

To visit the approach light, backtrack to the intersection with Hwy. 42 (Bridge St). Turn left (west) onto Hwy. 42 and go about 0.3 miles (0.48 km) to Chatham St. (Elgin County 39), the second street after crossing the bridge. Turn left (south) onto Chatham and drive about 0.8 miles (1.2 km) to a dirt road just before the sewage treatment plant. Turn left (east) and follow that road around to the right and into the parking area. You can view the approach light from the south end of the parking area

Port Stanley Breakwater Range Light

The Port Stanley Breakwater Range Light sits at the end of a short concrete pier that juts out into Lake Erie. Its square base extends the width of the pier, then narrows sharply upward to support a small rail with a green beacon at its tip. A small square room protrudes from the base of the light, and a long radio antenna that extends above the beacon helps guide ships during low or zero visibility.

Along the shore, Pierside Park offers a swimming beach with a lifeguard on duty and plenty of space to spread a picnic lunch or simply relax.

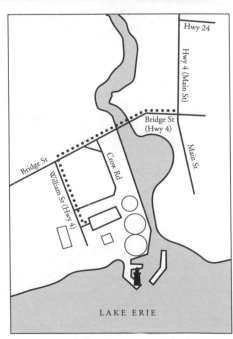

DIRECTIONS: From St. Thomas take Hwy. 4 south approximately 9.1 miles (13.9 km.) to Bridge St. in Port Stanley. Turn right (west) onto Bridge (following Hwy. 4) and go about 0.1 miles (0.16 km) to William St., the third street on the left after crossing the drawbridge. Turn left onto William (still following Hwy. 4) and go 0.4 miles (0.64 km) to its end, near the water. You can park in this area and view the pierhead light, to the left.

Rondeau West Breakwater and East Pierhead Lights

" On the lake side, the struc-ture's base curves deeply toward the water, giving the appear-ance of a canoe suddenly shoved ashore. "

At the end of a battered stone and concrete pier is the Rondeau West Breakwater Light. The tower's unusually shaped, massive concrete walls give it a unique profile. The wall facing shore is ordinary enough — flat and broken only by a door and small window high up its face — as it tapers slightly on its twenty-foot rise. But on the lake side, the struc-ture's base curves deeply toward the water, giving the appearance of a canoe sud-denly shoved ashore. In winter, layer upon layer of ice rise up this curve until you cannot distinguish between the ice shell and the concrete wall it encases.

Across the channel on a narrower pier, the Rondeau East Pierhead Light rises as a two-story white steel skeleton that holds a square, red lantern room. A steel walkway surrounds the lantern room, and large windows on each of its sides open to the blue expanse of Lake Erie.

Near the piers on Mariner Drive is Kenterieau Beach Park, a narrow, shady strip of land stretching along the shore. The park offers changing rooms for swimmers, restrooms, and a picnic pavilion.

RONDEAU EAST PIERHEAD LIGHT

RONDEAU WEST BREAKWATER LIGHT

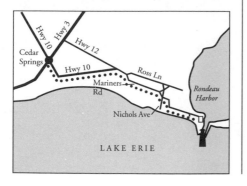

▋ DIRECTIONS: From the junction of Hwy. 3 and Kent County Road 10 in Cedar Springs (southwest of Blenheim near Lake Erie), turn south onto Co. Rd. 10 and follow it approxi-mately 1.6 miles (2.6 km) to the village of Erie Beach. Continue on Co. Rd. 10 another 3.4 miles (5.5 km) to the junction with Highway 12. Turn right (east) and go one mile (1.6 km) to where the road divides. Follow Mariners Rd., the one-way road on the right, 0.6 miles (0.96 km) to Nichols Ave. Turn right (south) onto Nichols and go one block to where the road turns left and is again named Mariners Rd. Follow Mariners Rd. 0.5 miles (0.80 km) to its end at Kenterleau Heritage Beach Park. Park anywhere along the roadway and walk to the end of Mariners Rd., then turn right and walk out along the pier. Or you can walk across the beach to the pier.

When you leave the area, from the junction of Kent County roads 10 and 12 west of Erieau, you can continue straight ahead on County Rd. 12 about 4.6 miles (7.4 km) back to Highway 3.

Southeast Shoal Lighthouse

The Southeast Shoal Light rises up out of Lake Erie seven miles south of Point Pelee. Because of its isolated location, it was often called "Little Alcatraz" by those who were assigned there. Its huge concrete foundation is protected by a large pile of rough stones, and as the white foundation rises, it narrows slightly. The square, white lighthouse rests atop that platform, leaving just enough room for a narrow walkway and red railing to surround it. The two-story building is topped by a smaller third level, and above that a helicopter pad provides Coast Guard access to the site. A jumble of modern improvements — red-and-white skeleton towers, steel stairways, antennaes and solar panels — give this light a unique space-age appearance.

"Because of its isolated location, this light was often called 'Little Alcatraz' by those who were assigned there."

Pelee Passage Light

"The structure has an unbalanced look, as though it should topple over."

The Pelee Passage Light marks the channel between Pelee Island and Point Pelee on the Canadian mainland. A green steel pillar rises about 20 feet above the blue depths of the lake to support a wide platform that holds the one-story lighthouse. The white building's flat roof is a helicopter landing pad, which is the only access to the station. The bright-green parapet and lantern room is supported by a narrow steel cylinder that stretches up 30 feet from one corner of the landing pad, giving the entire structure an unbalanced look, as though it should topple over.

Pelee Island Lighthouse Ruins

Pelee Island, located nine miles south of the Canadian coast and eight miles north of United States-owned Kelly's Island, has long been renowned for its winery and thriving tourist industry. Native North Americans were here first, however, as evidenced by scattered prehistoric manmade earthen mounds. There were many more, but the first European settlers obliterated most of the sacred grounds by plowing them under. The new arrivals turned other areas of the predominantly marshy island into arable land by constructing a system of canals, dykes and pumps that diverted unwanted water out into Lake Erie. Today, the island's rich earth still produces cash crops, mainly tobacco and soy beans.

The lighthouse was built in 1833 on a secluded section of the north shoreline now called Lighthouse Point. Its gray stone tower, long abandoned, now stands alone on the sandy beach, its strength still apparent despite the dark holes of missing windows and the absence of its lantern room and door. A single oak rises up alongside, its branches stretching above the structure, and a metal gate over the tower entrance keeps visitors out.

The surrounding beach is a beautiful place to explore or wade in the water. In a marsh behind the light, a grove of long-dead tree trunks protrude from the water, their surface bleached white by the elements.

A committee has been established to help maintain the light, and their long-term goal is complete restoration. If you would like to contact them, write Relight the Lighthouse Committee, Attn: Don Hanes, Pelee Island, Ontario, Canada NOR 1MO.

> *The gray stone tower stands alone on the sandy beach, its strength still apparent despite the dark holes of missing windows and the absence of its lantern room and door.*

DIRECTIONS: You can make the one-hour trip to Pelee Island on an auto ferry from either Leamington or Kingsville. For further information call 1-800-661-2220 or write Pelee Island Transportation, Pelee Island, Ontario NOR 1MO.

Once on the island, from the ferry dock turn left (northeast) onto Scudder Road (which bears left past a metal building, then turns to gravel) and go 0.7 miles (1.1 km) to the point where the route curves sharply right (southeast) and becomes Clutton Rd. Follow Clutton for 0.1 mile (.16 km) to Harris-Garno Rd. (just past the entry road to the quarry). Turn left (east) onto Harris-Garno and go 0.8 miles (1.2 km) to the tee intersection at Lighthouse Dr. (East Shore Dr.). Turn left (north) and follow the road about 0.6 miles (0.96 km) to its end. Park and then follow the well-worn trail from the road's end about one block to a sign that points the way to the lighthouse, to the right. Follow the path a short distance to the beach, then turn left and walk down the shore to the lighthouse, in view about two blocks away. The entire walk is about ¼ mile (0.5 km), one way.

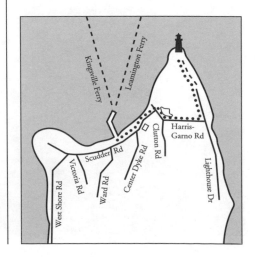

PELEE ISLAND LIGHTHOUSE RUINS

Leamington Light

The Leamington light is a three-story, white wooden structure with a square base gradually tapering upwards. Eight-paned windows protrude slightly on each side of the tower, and a thick, square walkway surrounds the brick-red parapet. The light is on private property in the middle of a subdivision, but you can view it from Seacliff Park.

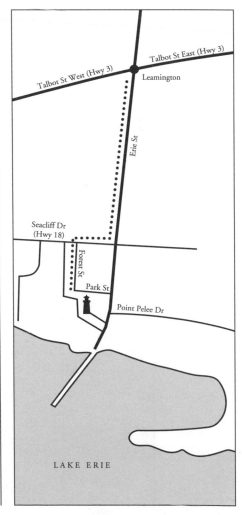

DIRECTIONS: From Hwy. 3 (Talbot St.) in downtown Leamington, turn south onto Erie St. (Hwy. 18) and go approximately 1.3 miles (2.1 km) to Seacliff Dr. Turn right (west) onto Seacliff (still following Hwy. 18) and drive about 0.2 miles (0.32 km) to Forest St. Turn left (south) onto Forest and go about two blocks to its end, at Park St. You can park in this area and walk through the park grounds to a fence from where you can get a good view of the lighthouse, which is on private property. When you leave this area, you can go east on Park St. to return to Erie St. To visit the lakefront area, turn right (south) onto Erie; to return to Hwy. 3, turn left (north).

113

Kingsville Light

The Kingsville Light has been moved from its original location near the lake and is now in a private storage area on Lansdowne Avenue. Sections of its wooden siding are missing, and boards along the second-story walkway have been removed. The black lantern is still surrounded by triangle-shaped panes of glass.

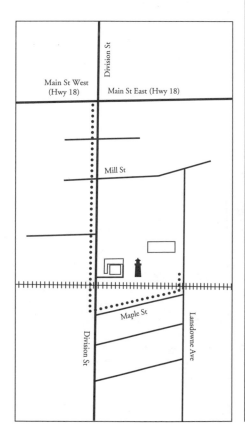

DIRECTIONS: From Hwy. 18 in Kingsville, turn south onto Division St. and go about six blocks to Maple St. (just across the railroad tracks). Turn left (east) onto Maple and go one block to Lansdowne Ave. Turn left (north) onto Lansdowne. You get good views of the light, on the left, as you drive down Maple and just after you cross the railroad tracks on Lansdowne.

Boblo Island Lighthouse

The Boblo Island Lighthouse rests near the Detroit River's edge on a small bluff covered with deep-green bushes that trail down to the water. The white paint is nearly worn off the tower's weathered brick sides, and at the parapet, both railing and lantern room have long since disappeared. A square 12-paned window high up the river side of the three-story tower provides the only illumination to the interior.

Boblo Island is the site of a huge, popular amusement park that attracts thousands each day throughout the summer months. But the light is in a relaxing, secluded area well-away from the boisterous section. Plus the continued operation of the park is in uncertain.

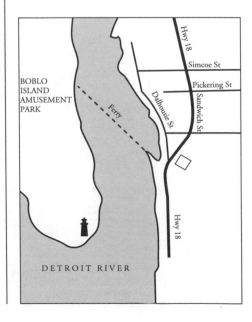

DIRECTIONS: From the intersection of Hwy. 18 (Sandwich St.) and Pickering St. on the south edge of Amherstburg, go south on Hwy. 18 about 0.7 miles (1.1 km) to the parking area for the Bob-Lo Island Amusement Park, on the left. Continue on Hwy. 18 another 0.3 miles (0.5 km), stop, and view the light, on the right, across the river on Boblo Island.

For a closeup look, take the ferry to the island and make your way to the southeast side, near the Historic Blockhouse.

115

Colchester Reef Light

F our miles offshore from the small town of Colchester, a light was built in 1885 to warn mariners of a dangerous reef beneath the waters of Lake Erie. Today, the remnants of the original stone tower stretch up only 10 feet from the aging concrete foundation. The old structure ends abruptly at a small, modern helicopter pad, with a 15-foot-tall skeleton tower rising from one corner to a red light at its peak.

Old Pelee Passage Light

The Old Pelee Passage Light has been moved from its offshore home (between Pelee Island and Point Pelee) to Lakeview Park in Windsor. The white metal siding of the tower is interrupted only by a few square windows. The bright-red parapet, surrounded by a decorative curved railing, supports a 10-sided red lantern room.

DIRECTIONS: From the corner of Highway 3-B (Ouelette Ave.) and Riverside Dr., near the Detroit-Windsor Tunnel entrance in Windsor, go east (upstream) on Riverside about 5.7 miles (9.2 km) to Lakeview Park, on the left. The Old Pelee Passage Light is next to the river in the park.

Thames River Rear Range Lighthouse

"A mist of bushy green sur-rounds the light as trees and grasses bend to the leisurely flowing river."

Where the Thames River empties into Lake St. Clair, a small light-house guards the surrounding waters. The Thames River Rear Range Light, at Lighthouse Cove near Tilbury, is a 40-foot-high, round brick tower, with a few windows set deeply into the stone. The top half of the tower is much smoother than the bottom, but a heavy coat of white paint blends the two sections. Window trim is red, matching the octagonal parapet and 10-sided lantern room above.

A mist of bushy green surrounds the light as trees and grasses bend to the leisurely flowing river. And there's plenty of room to spread a picnic lunch.

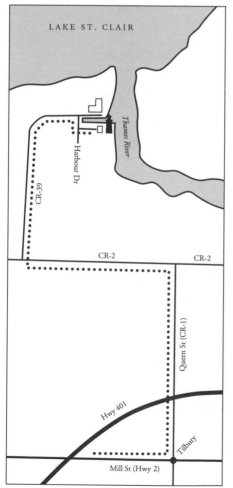

DIRECTIONS: From Hwy. 401 about 25 miles (40 km) east of Windsor, exit (#56) onto Mills St. (Hwy. 2) and go 1.4 miles (2.2 km) to Queen St. (County Rd. 1) in Tilbury. Turn left (north) onto Queen and drive about 2.8 miles (4.5 km) to County Road 2. Turn left (west) onto Co. Rd. 2 and go 2.1 miles (3.3 km) to County Road 39. Turn right (north) onto Co. Rd. 39 and go 2.4 miles (3.8 km) to Harbour Dr., a gravel road. Turn right (east) onto Harbour and look for a canal on the left. Just past the canal, turn left onto a narrow road and park in a small area on the left side. The old lighthouse is a short distance beyond the parking area.

Corunna Rear Range Light

I n 1890 a 33-foot-high wooden tower was erected to serve as a rear range light in the small town of Corunna. It assisted ships along this section of the St. Clair River until 1941, when it was taken out of service. Although the Coast Guard had announced no plans to demolish the light, the citizens of Corunna didn't want to give them the opportunity. They purchased the light from the Coast Guard for $75 and kept it safe for the next 10 years.

But in 1951 the Coast Guard repurchased the light, refurbished it (including converting to electric power), and put it into service for another 31 years. Then again, in 1982, the Coast Guard decided that the light was outdated and needed to be replaced. Too many trees had grown in front of the tower, blocking the view of the light from the river. A new 50-foot-high steel tower was built nearby and the original wooden structure was scheduled for demolition.

But the townspeople of Corunna stepped in and saved their light again. This time they moved it four miles south to a museum at Mooretown, also on the St. Clair River. There, the tower's square base tapers upward to support a small

light and larger uniquely shaped red-and-white day marker. Also on the grounds are a log cabin, a Victorian cottage, and a railroad station and old schoolhouse that are currently being restored. The museum's main building encloses several rooms filled with local antiques and artifacts, and one room is devoted to a nautical theme.

A beautiful parkway — with more than a dozen quiet, shady parks practically within touching distance of passing freighters — follows the river in the Mooretown/Corunna area. And a car ferry between Marine City, Michigan, and Sombra, Ontario, is an interesting way to reach the area.

"A beautiful parkway — with more than a dozen quiet, shady parks practically within touching distance of passing freighters — follows the river in the Mooretown/Corunna area."

DIRECTIONS: From the St. Clair Parkway (Lambton County Road 33) in Mooretown, turn east onto William St. (Moore Rd. 6) and go three blocks to the Mooretown Museum, on the left.

119

ALPHABETICAL LISTING OF LIGHTHOUSES

Lighthouses You Can Enter

Lighthouses Whose Towers You Can Climb

Lighthouse Museums

Lighthouses That Are Still Active

CHARTERS

In several instances we used charter services to reach lighthouses located a great distance from land.

We used two different charter boat services and highly recommend both. Prices are reasonable, and the friendly captains are knowledgable about the history of their areas.

Thousand Islands, New York area (Rock Island, Sunken Rock, Sisters Island and Crossover Island lights):

Joshua M. Historical Boat Tours
22 Otter Street
Alexandria Bay, NY 13607
(315) 482-6415.
Ask for Captain Berny Coffey or his wife, Valerie. (And when out on the boat, be sure to ask what the "M" stands for!)

Port Colborne and Point Abino (Ontario) areas (Port Colborne, Mohawk Island and Point Abino lights):

Brenda C Charters
Primo's Restaurant
225 Main Street West
Port Colborne, Ontario L3K 3V7
(416) 835-8281.
Ask for Captain Primo Macoritto or his wife, Brenda.

We have also used and can recommend the following charter air services:

Isle of Quinte and eastern Lake Ontario Islands:

Loyal-Air Ltd.
Belleville, Ontario
(613) 962-0124

The northern shore of Lake Erie and the Long Point area:

St. Thomas Aviation
St. Thomas, Ontario
(519) 631-1031

Sackets Harbor and Horse Island areas of New York

Brouty Aviation
Watertown Airport
Dexter, NY
(315) 639-6606

Pigeon Island Light

BIBLIOGRAPHY

Ahern, Frances Robin. *Oakville, A Small Town*. Erin, Ontario: Boston Mills Press, 1981.

Articles from Cleveland Plain Dealer.

Baird, David M. "Lighthouses of Canada." *Canadian Geographic*, June/July 1982, pp. 44-53.

"Coast Guard Opens Probe of Boat Crash Against Lighthouse." *Buffalo News*, July 28, 1958.

"Coast Guard to Give Lighthouse to State Park." *Erie Morning News*, November 4, 1988.

Cruickshank, Tom, and Peter Jon Stokes. *The Settler's Dream*. Picton, Ontario: Corporation of the County of Prince Edward, 1954.

Deckert, Dick. "Little House on the Peninsula." *Erie Times-News*, December 29, 1974.

DeLuca, Helen R. *The Lake Erie Isles and How They Got Their Names*. for Historic Lyme Church Association, 1974.

Dunnigan, Brian Leight. *A History and Guide to Old Fort Niagara*. Youngstown, New York: Old Fort Niagara Association, Inc., 1985.

Emery, Claire, and Barbara Ford. *From Pathway to Skyway: A History of Burlington*. Confederation Committee of Burlington, Ontario.

Hart, Cheryl. "The Queen's Wharf Lighthouse." *The Beacon*, Fall 1986, pp. 3-4.

A History of Fairport Harbor, Ohio. Fairport Harbor Bicentennial Committee, Painsville, Ohio: Lake Photo Engraving, Inc. 1976.

"Landmark Lighthouse in Limbo." *The Erie Story Magazine*. April, 1976.

"Lighthouse: Landmarks in Lake's Lantern Lore." *The Erie Story*, September, 1972, pp. 6-12.

Ligibel, Ted, and Richard Wright. *Island Heritage: A Guided Tour to Lake Erie's Bass Islands*, Ohio State University Press, 1987.

Loverseed, Helga V. *Burlington: An Illustrated History*. Burlington, Ontario: Windsor Publications, 1988.

Malkus, Alida. *Blue Water Boundary: Epic Highway of the Great Lakes and the St. Lawrence*. New York: Hastings House, 1960.

Marryman, J. H. *The United States Life Saving Service — 1880*. Grand Junction, Colorado: Vista Books, 1989.

Metcalfe, Willis. *Sing of Sailors: Canvas and Steam on Quinte Waters*. Picton, Ontario: The Picton Gazette Publishing Co. Ltd., 1965.

McKinney, Bill. "Erie Landmark Needs Caretaker." *Erie Morning News*, November 8, 1993.

McQuaid, Deborah. "Erie's Lighthouses Beckons Tour Group." *Erie Times-News*, September 15, 1990.

"The Old Charlotte Light." *Upstate Magazine*, June 3, 1984.

"Presque Isle Lighthouse Has Been Home to Many." *Erie Times News*, August 29, 1993.

Prothero, Frank and Nancy. *Memories: A History of Port Burwell*.

Reuter, Bob. *Put-In-Bay Self-Guided Tour*. Put-In-Bay, Ohio: CGH Limited Inc., 1992.

Russ, Jean Madigan. *Point Gratiot's Guiding Light: The Dunkirk Light Station*. Falconer, New York: Falconer Printing and Design Inc., 1986.

Special Collections, Great Lakes Lighthouse Society Reference Library, Vermilion, Ohio.

Special Collections, St. Catherines Public Library, St. Catherines, Ontario, Canada.

Special Collections, Toledo-Lucas County Public Library, Toledo, Ohio.

Stone, Dave. *Long Point: Last Port of Call*. Erin, Ontario: Boston Mills Press, 1988.

Tinney, James, and Mary Burdette-Watkins, with Leo Kuschel, Illustrator. *Seaway Trail Lighthouses: An Illustrated Guide to the Lighthouses Along New York State's Great Lakes, Niagara and St. Lawrence Rivers*. Oswego, New York: Seaway Trail, Inc., 1989.

Marblehead Lighthouse

THE AUTHORS

The Penrose family resides in rural West Branch, Michigan. Bill, 54, has worked for the Pepsi Cola Company for 28 years. He enjoys exploring and photographing Michigan with his wife, Ruth, 53, who works full time as an X-ray technician in their home area.

Their daughter Laurie, 31, has taken a break from teaching to devote full time to her and husband Ross' two children, Masina, 5, and Alex, 2. Bill Penrose Jr., 25, is hard at work transforming the thousands of Michigan outdoor photographs the Penroses have taken over the years into a viable family business.

This is the Penroses' third family-effort book. *A Guide to 199 Michigan Waterfalls* was published in 1988, and *A Traveler's Guide to 116 Michigan Lighthouses* was published in 1992.